AMERICAN HIGHER EDUCATION AND WORLD AFFAIRS

Studies in Universities and World Affairs—

AMERICAN COLLEGE LIFE AS EDUCATION IN WORLD OUTLOOK
Howard E. Wilson

FOREIGN STUDENTS AND HIGHER EDUCATION IN THE UNITED STATES
Cora Du Bois

THE UNIVERSITY, THE CITIZEN, AND WORLD AFFAIRS
Cyril O. Houle and Charles A. Nelson

TRAINING OF SPECIALISTS IN INTERNATIONAL RELATIONS
C. Dale Fuller

INTERNATIONAL RELATIONS IN INSTITUTIONS OF HIGHER EDUCATION IN THE SOUTH
Fred Cole

UNIVERSITY RESEARCH ON INTERNATIONAL AFFAIRS
John Gange

WORLD AFFAIRS AND THE COLLEGE CURRICULUM
Richard N. Swift

AMERICAN HIGHER EDUCATION AND WORLD AFFAIRS
Howard E. Wilson and Florence H. Wilson

American Higher Education and World Affairs

HOWARD E. WILSON
Dean, School of Education
University of California, Los Angeles

and

FLORENCE H. WILSON

AMERICAN COUNCIL ON EDUCATION · *Washington, D.C.*

Prepared for the Carnegie Endowment for International Peace; published by the American Council on Education

United Nations Plaza at 46th Street
New York 17, New York

LIBRARY OF CONGRESS CATALOG CARD NO. 63-18785

PRINTED IN THE UNITED STATES OF AMERICA

Foreword

THIS VOLUME by Howard E. and Florence H. Wilson brings to a conclusion an inquiry initiated by the Carnegie Endowment in 1950. In the last quarter century, the United States has found itself increasingly caught up in the complexities of international affairs. Not least to be affected by this radical change, which has permeated the whole of American society, have been our institutions of higher education. "Scholars' concerns," say the Wilsons, "have a new value in the market place of polity, and the vexing questions of society, a new relevance to academic disciplines."

Because changes have intervened so rapidly and because the university's responsibility in the public domain has increased so sharply, centers of learning have been faced with major problems of reorganization and revision to meet today's challenge. The Endowment's program, as the authors point out, was designed to "help colleges and universities to think through the problems and possibilities inherent in their relation to world affairs."

The first part of this program was the promotion of a series of self-inventories in American universities. Between 1951 and 1954, representatives from some 300 colleges and universities participated in conferences organized under Endowment auspices, and some 70 engaged in self-appraisals of their resources and academic activities bearing on world affairs. The second part of the program was a series of volumes dealing with various facets of the role of universities in international affairs. Mr. and Mrs. Wilson's concluding volume brings together the threads of the preceding studies. Their primary emphasis, however, is not so much on summary as on analysis of institutional policy and of administrative organization by which policy may be implemented. Since the Endowment's pioneering enterprise there have been both a growing concern with this field and a number of studies and reports, of which *The University and World Affairs* is perhaps the best known. Mr. and Mrs. Wilson have drawn heavily upon these in the preparation of the present volume.

The Wilsons' thesis is that "each college or university needs, at this stage, to inventory its resources and activities and experiences bearing on world affairs, to formulate with clarity its policies respecting developments of the proximate future with a view to what and how much the institution should do, and to provide an institutional structure . . . which will coordinate the university's undertakings, continually appraise its activities, and be the focal point for continuing re-examination of policies and programs." Mr. and Mrs. Wilson see a major role for the new organization, Education and World Affairs, which was established in 1962: "to mobilize the resources of the educational community in the fullest possible development of American competence in world affairs"; it can provide guidelines and raise questions for the continuing consideration of individual institutions.

The Carnegie Endowment is deeply indebted to the American Council on Education, which has published this series of volumes for us. The Council's decision to undertake that task and the effective way it has done so are excellent testimony of its continuing interest in the promotion of international cultural relations through institutions of higher learning.

I also wish to express the Endowment's appreciation to the authors of this series—Fred Cole, Cora Du Bois, C. Dale Fuller, John Gange, Cyril O. Houle, Charles A. Nelson, Richard N. Swift, Florence H. Wilson—and particularly to Howard E. Wilson for his combined role as inspirer and organizer of the program, editor of this series, and author or coauthor of two of the volumes. Mr. Wilson brought to his task a wide range of experience and maturity of judgment. He has taught at Harvard University, edited the *Harvard Educational Review,* directed for eight years the Endowment's activities in the area of education and world affairs, and served as executive secretary of the Educational Policies Commission of the National Education Association, chairman of the Education Commission of the National Conference of Christians and Jews, director of the Unesco Seminar on International Education, and American consultant to the Turkish National Commission on Education. Since 1957 Mr. Wilson has been dean of the School of Education at the University of California, Los Angeles.

In this, as in other volumes of the series, the opinions expressed are those of the authors and not necessarily those of the Carnegie Endowment for International Peace, but the Endowment can testify to the scholarly and thoughtful approach that makes this volume not only a capstone to its own program but a worthy contribution to the ever-growing literature in the field.

JOSEPH E. JOHNSON, *President*
Carnegie Endowment for International Peace

Preface

THE AUTHORS of this volume acknowledge with deep appreciation their indebtedness to many persons who have aided in its preparation. Francis Brown, of the staff of the American Council on Education, helped plan the book, and we had hoped for his coauthorship, but his untimely death prevented this. The staff members of the Carnegie Endowment and of the American Council on Education, as well as many other friends in governmental or foundation or academic positions have contributed much to the authors. Yet, with all their help, the volume's shortcomings are our own.

HOWARD AND FLORENCE WILSON

Contents

List of Tables

1

Higher Education in Twentieth-Century Society

HAD SOME ACADEMIC Jules Verne predicted in 1900 the changes that have come to American colleges and universities since that time under the impact of world affairs, he would have appeared more ridiculous to most of his colleagues than the real Jules Verne seemed to be in *Around the World in Eighty Days.* By the same token, the way that academic interests and competencies now influence foreign policy would have seemed impossible to diplomats at the turn of the century. The relations among nations, and the roster of nations, have changed radically since the seeming security of the Victorian era, and these changes have affected all human institutions in all countries, including the institutions devoted to higher education. The changes in American colleges and universities already recorded within this century under the impact of world affairs demonstrate the validity of Abraham Flexner's observation thirty years ago that

> A university, like all other human institutions—like church, like governments, like philanthropic organizations—is not outside, but inside the general social fabric of a given era . . . It is . . . an expression of the age, as well as an influence operating upon both present and future.[1]

Impact of World Affairs on Academic Matters

Developments in American interests and responsibilities in world affairs since the 1890's have outmoded and overwhelmed

[1] Abraham Flexner, *Universities: American, English, German* (New York: Oxford University Press, 1930), p. 3.

our nineteenth-century isolation. The United States, in some respects unwilling and unready, has in other respects functioned as "an arsenal of democracy" in the international tensions of the twentieth century. The century has certainly not been a calm one, nor is calmness now in prospect. Change has accelerated in geometric progression, with inevitable struggles of an ideological nature, with the rise of new nations, and with the rising expectations of vast populations. In a sense, it is once again such an era of expansion and exploration, controversy and creativity as that which marked the years of Columbus and Shakespeare, Elizabeth and Philip II, Galileo and Newton. In such a burgeoning complex of societies and ideas and interests and conflicts, the United States moves into the center of world affairs—and with the nation move its colleges and universities. The same forces that have developed a Department of State so different as to be hardly recognizable from the Department of the 1890's have already developed colleges and universities markedly different from those of 1900—the period which Canby described as the "Gothic Age" of American colleges.[2]

Certain changes which have emerged in recent decades in the interrelations among states have special relevance to the interests and characteristic responsibilities of institutions of higher education. The shrinking globe, for example, involves not only a reduction of the time required for transportation and communication of men and ideas, but, even more strikingly, an increase in the varieties of cultures which come into close contact with each other. In his Preface to *The Dark Side of the Moon,* T. S. Eliot wrote:

> . . . before 1914 the balance of power, together with the initiative, lay between states which had a long common history, and a certain common heritage of traditions, states which had had relations with each other—though only fitfully friendly relations—since their beginnings. Their political exchanges were not carried on without trickery and

[2] Henry Seidel Canby, *Alma Mater: The Gothic Age of the American College* (New York: Farrar & Rinehart, 1936).

deceit: but when politicians lied, they lied in the same terms; when they were guilty of hypocrisy . . . it was the same God whose name they took in vain. Hence there was always a great deal that could be taken for granted. . . . [Now] the great powers and the nascent powers stretch all over the globe and comprehend a great variety of types of culture; issues between them extend deeper than ever before, and offer possibilities of much greater misunderstandings.[3]

The complexities of cooperation or coexistence or conflict among states of widely varying nature and values and mores are extraordinarily and increasingly great. Both the assumptions and the customary procedures among those seated at an international conference table today are elusively diverse. It becomes more difficult to confer and, at the same time, the urgencies of war and peace make conferring essential and almost continuous. To sit at the conference table or to develop and implement and support an insightful foreign policy, twentieth-century men have to master a variety of foreign languages that were once relatively unimportant. And back of those languages lie whole societies whose histories and governments and economics and problems and aspirations must be comprehended by those who confer constructively. The whole network of intercommunication among nations involves the accumulation of knowledge—knowledge of peoples and nations, of value systems and motivations—previously beyond the horizons of the centers of power. Reductions of global distance and time are basically significant because they reveal social distances and cultural lags which must be bridged if the total society is to function well.

This infinite variety of cultures and values and the means by which communication and understanding among them may be effected lie directly within the concerns of academic men. The established disciplines of the social sciences and humanities have their focus on the vast "tangled web" of human relations, but until recently the concern has been largely limited to a European tradition. Now it must embrace the world. There are

[3] New York: Charles Scribner's Sons, 1947, pp. viii–ix.

today furious academic efforts to stretch the horizons over the non-Western world. Foreign policy for all modern nations draws upon the knowledge and insights which have been the traditional concerns of academia, and new forces or new emphases operate within higher education under the incessant impact of our widening international horizons.

A second factor of world politics particularly influential on education is the ideological conflict which has created two poles of political thought, two centers of philosophical outlook and of political power, with the possibility of a neutral force or forces between them. In a period in which "ideas are weapons" and international politics derive much of their character from differing concepts of life, it is inevitable that universities are closely involved. From the query of Christopher Fry's baffled sixteenth-century magistrate's wife, "What in the world have world affairs to do with anything?"[4] we have moved into an era of inquiry into the relation of world affairs to economic growth and development, social welfare, health, education, and the great philosophical questions of freedom and justice. The intellectual and esthetic queries about life, with which universities have traditionally been concerned, are now caught up vigorously in the ferment of international life. Scholars' concerns have a new value in the market place of polity, and the vexing questions of society, a new relevance to academic disciplines.

Academic interests and public interests are further intermeshed by the current scientific-technological revolution, particularly as this is related to questions of security and national defense. Nuclear fission is but the most dramatic instance of the marriage of scholarly interests and national needs in a period of scientific advance and international uncertainty. Research programs governmentally financed in American universities have altered significantly the relations between government and

[4] Christopher Fry, *The Lady's Not for Burning* (New York: Oxford University Press, 1954), p. 45.

higher education and the relations of scholarly disciplines within the curriculum. As, under the demands of preparedness and defense, the natural sciences have flourished, old concepts of a liberal education have changed. In contemporary times the natural sciences lie close to the center of liberalizing studies. Research has taken on a new emphasis and a new character in universities; laboratories are now as much a symbol of the university as are libraries. Vast funds from the public treasury go into the university tasks of training and retraining scientific specialists, of research ranging from atomic physics to automatic computation. Universities are increasingly caught up in programs of national development—for economic prosperity, political viability, and esthetic quality—in underdeveloped areas, the emerging nations of the world. The rapidity and the universality with which scientific and technological development, accelerated by international tension and financed heavily from governmental funds, have modified the traditions and practices of academic life, in America and elsewhere, are difficult to comprehend but are of the utmost academic and political significance.

Another aspect of international relations, closely related to contact among diverse cultures, to ideological conflict, and to scientific advance, is the degree to which, during this century, scholarly and cultural and educational matters have themselves become instruments of foreign policy. Early in the twentieth century, the government of France established a cultural relations unit in the Ministry on the Quai d'Orsay and began to utilize the establishment of French schools abroad, the foreign distribution of French books and magazines, and the export of operas, ballets, concerts, and lectures as part of French foreign policy. By the advent of World War I various governments had established information services to increase foreign understanding of their national cultures and policies, and the lines between cultural relations and propaganda were often blurred. Under the League of Nations, the Institute of Intellectual Cooperation was established as a part of the machinery of international action. After World War I, the United Kingdom set up the British Council, a semiautonomous governmental agency which established British Houses in the principal cities of Europe and Asia, arranged tours for British theatrical groups, maintained libraries, and furthered the teaching of English. In the years following both World War I and World War II, cultural activities of this nature became increasingly matters of concern and responsibility among all governments.[5] National programs of international cultural relations became commonplace, though often awkwardly and reluctantly developed.

In 1938 the United States created a small cultural relations office in the Department of State, the predecessor of agencies concerned with Latin American cultural relations, of the United States Information Service, of programs devoted to interchange of persons, of the appointment, two decades later, of an Assistant Secretary for Cultural Affairs in the Department of State. By the 1960's some thousands of employees and millions of dollars were involved in American programs of cultural relations abroad, as will be described in some detail in chapter 4 of this volume. The new role of "education, science, and culture" in international affairs was evidenced in the rapid establishment of Unesco as a Specialized Agency of the United Nations in 1946 and in bilateral cultural treaties such as that signed by the United States and the Soviet Union in 1958.

Two-way traffic between academic classroom and government office became commonplace during the 1940's and 1950's. Hardly a campus in the United States in the 1960's is without a returned Fulbright scholar, or a former cultural attaché in a United States Embassy, or an ex-employee of the United States Information

[5] For an early, brief summary of these developments, see Ruth McMurray and Muna Lee, *The Cultural Approach: Another Way in International Relations* (Chapel Hill: University of North Carolina Press, 1948); "National Programs of International Cultural Relations: A Seminar Report," *International Conciliation,* No. 462 (June 1950), pp. 301–36.

Service or the Agency for International Development among its faculty. These scholars, from a wide range of disciplines, have brought a new academic element into the foreign operations of the government and have carried home to their campuses a new experience of reality to add to the conversations of campus and classroom. These members of the academic community have contributed substantially to the kinds of campus adjustments to international affairs which are discussed in the second and third chapters of this volume. Their participation in the conduct of a foreign policy encompassing their scholarly and professional specialties increased the participation of higher education generally in the actualities of international affairs.

All these facets of international relations—the multiplication of cultures and viewpoints in international contacts, the ideological tensions among modern nations, the acceleration of scientific developments and their relation to national defense, the rising role of cultural affairs as elements of foreign policy—introduce new forces, new tensions, new potentialities into every nation's institutions of higher education. In the United States, their influence has been particularly strong because of the pragmatic conviction in our tradition that wisdom emerges when knowledge is applied to action. The "service function" which, in addition to the functions of research and teaching, is so strong a motif in American academic life has encouraged interrelations between American universities, the United States Government, and world affairs. Such interrelations derived from the nature of contemporary international life take on added and poignant significance for universities as seen against the background of two world wars which drew their costliest casualties from the student bodies of higher education.

The universities, in view of their academic population, financing, freedom of inquiry, and purpose of preserving the intellectual and esthetic achievements of the humane traditions, also have their own concerns in international relations. These are reflected in the increasing interchanges of students and faculties and research specialists across national boundaries, in the expanding calendar of international conferences on scholarly and professional subjects, in the growing number of international associations formed by scholars and by students, in the establishment since World War II of such organizations as the International Association of Universities.

Adjustments under the impact of influences derived from the international situation have been continuous in American colleges and universities since the rise of the United States to a major role in world affairs. These adjustments appear in every segment and area of academia—in the enrollment of students, in recruitment of faculty members and provision for their leaves of absence, in financing for institutions both public and private, in the rise of new curriculum concerns and the shift of scholarly emphases, in the rise of a new field of international relations, in a new interest in languages, in the unprecedented expansion of research, in extracurricular activities for students, in university governance.

Extraordinary academic achievements among these areas of adjustment are a part of the record of American higher education in recent decades. Reception of foreign students and scholars, establishment of area study centers, acceptance of university contracts for work abroad are indicative of these achievements. But it is also true that many of the developments within individual colleges or universities have been made on a piecemeal basis, in a series of uncoordinated efforts, and often without conscientious analysis of purposes and of appropriate responsibilities. Some institutions in the United States have overexpanded themselves under the stimulus of high motives unanalyzed critically in terms of institutional responsibilities and resources. Some institutions, adhering to more rigid traditions, have failed to envisage the college or university in its relation to twentieth-century society. In many colleges and universities a variety of programs and developments, individually legitimate, are wastefully uncoordinated. Very few institutions of higher education have anything remotely resembling a master plan for academic action in relation to the multiplying influences derived from international matters.

Adjustments in academic institutions to the burgeoning activities of relations among modern states continue at an accelerating pace. To consolidate the academic advances already achieved, to profit from past errors, to make further developments with increasing wisdom, it is but common sense for American institutions of higher learning to take stock of what is happening, to establish criteria for further adjustments, to formulate a philosophy and policy in accord with current responsibilities. Analysis of what has happened to universities under the impact of world affairs and what must be envisaged for the immediate future of higher education—the role of colleges and universities in a free society, of national policy respecting cultural affairs in foreign policy, and of careful planning for each individual institution—has now a high priority. It is to such an analysis that this volume is devoted.

The Carnegie Endowment Program on Universities and World Affairs

The considerations of this volume arise directly from a program of the Carnegie Endowment for International Peace, set against the background of the events and current trends of American life. The volume brings to a conclusion a program which the Carnegie Endowment for International Peace began in 1950, and which has now involved more than a decade of exploration of the interrelationships between American colleges and universities and the conduct of modern world affairs.

From the earliest years of its founding in 1911, the Endowment worked closely with American and European universities in facilitating exchange of professors, in helping develop the fields of international law and international relations, in supporting student international relations clubs, in financing research studies and publications contributory to the literature on war and peace, and on international action.

In raising questions about the best role of American universities in respect to the nation's responsibilities in international affairs, as it began to do in this program in 1950, the Endowment was in part analyzing its own history and searching for its best role under post-World War II conditions. In a deeper sense it was joining in a general appraisal of American higher education at the mid-point of the twentieth century. The Endowment's trustees and staff members were concerned with ascertaining more exactly the responsibilities of colleges and universities in the international field, with redefining liberal education in terms of twentieth-century demands, with exploring the new relations between government and universities—all of these conceived as bases for meeting adequately the challenges which assuredly lay ahead. The Endowment's program on "universities and world affairs" was not directed toward promoting some academic adjustments and negating others, but was essentially a call to colleges and universities to think through the problems and possibilities inherent in their relation to world affairs and to America's role in world affairs. The program was neither propaganda nor experimentation but basically a reaffirmation of the admonition to "know thyself" as applied to institutions of higher education in this particular context.

In 1950, nine American colleges or universities undertook, at the Endowment's request, to make relatively informal self-inventories of their activities, resources, problems, and possibilities as related to foreign policy and international relations. The essential purpose of this pilot enterprise was the identification of questions which institutions of higher education in the United States should be asking themselves at this juncture in history. At the suggestion of the Endowment, faculty committees were set up at the University of Denver, the University of Michigan, the University of Pittsburgh, New Jersey State Teachers College at Trenton, Columbia University, Vassar College, and Colgate University; during the spring of 1950 these committees, working with members of the Endowment staff, sought to identify queries appropriate for a self-study questionnaire. From their discussions emerged an instrument containing 95 questions grouped under ten topics: (1) basic objectives of higher education as related to world affairs, (2) influence of world affairs on general education at the college level, (3) interchange of students and faculty, (4) foreign students on American campuses, (5) the university role in adult education about world affairs, (6) university research on international relations, (7) training of specialists in international relations, (8) training an international civil service, (9) coordination of international programs within a university, and (10) relation of the institution to government, foundations, and other agencies concerned with international matters. During ensuing months each of the cooperating institutions made a preliminary self-analysis in terms of this list of questions, revising the appraisal instrument as they progressed.

In 1951 a report was published by the Carnegie Endowment on this exploratory experience—a report which indicated its purpose, presented the instrument of self-appraisal, and gave general comments on the findings resulting from its use in the nine cooperating institutions.[6] The publication was intended as a preliminary handbook, a device for encouraging American institutions of higher education individually to examine themselves in terms of the questions it raised. It was used as the basis for discussion at a series of regional conferences covering the United States, convened by the Endowment, to which some three hundred colleges and universities sent representatives. Between 1951 and 1953 such regional conferences were held in

[6] Howard E. Wilson, *Universities and World Affairs* (New York: Carnegie Endowment for International Peace, 1951).

Boston, New York, Philadelphia, Charlottesville, Atlanta, Dallas, Denver, Los Angeles, Berkeley, Portland, Minneapolis, Cleveland, and St. Louis. The institutions attending were not only those especially interested in international affairs, but a cross-section of America's colleges and universities—large and small, rural and urban, public and private. Significantly, the representatives attending the conferences included persons concerned with over-all administration and policy as well as specialists in international studies.

As a result of the discussions at these conferences, institutional self-studies were undertaken by a widely scattered, diverse group of American colleges and universities. By 1954, aided only by consultative and clearinghouse services from the Endowment, more than seventy institutions had completed self-studies. These studies varied greatly in scope and consequence, for the total enterprise as set up by the Endowment was thoroughly decentralized. It was not an effort to secure exact and comparative appraisals so much as a means of encouraging institutions to study themselves in relation to the international aspect of their surrounding society. The self-study reports were mimeographed by the Endowment, distributed among the cooperating institutions, and used as a basis for various consultations. Together, the reports, varying in length from six to three hundred pages, provided a comprehensive insight into the perplexities and aspirations of American higher education as it was adjusting itself to the many impacts arising from international affairs in the early 1950's.

As the institutional self-studies which had been encouraged by the Endowment neared completion, a series of particularly important topics were identified which were, or should be, of concern both to specialists in international relations and to the administrative policy makers of American colleges and universities. The Endowment then contracted with a number of specialists to prepare reports on these topics. Each report was to draw upon the seventy self-studies which had been completed but was not limited to them. Each was to take into consideration such other studies, researches, and publications as had relevance to its topic. The American Council on Education agreed to publish the series of volumes for the Endowment. Between 1955 and 1959 seven volumes were issued: *American College Life as Education in World Outlook* by Howard E. Wilson; *Foreign Students and Higher Education in the United States* by Cora Du Bois, now of the Harvard faculty; *Training of Specialists in International Relations* by C. Dale Fuller, now of the Foreign Policy Association; *University Research on International Affairs* by John Gange, now of the University of Oregon; *The University, The Citizen, and World Affairs* by Cyril O. Houle, of the University of Chicago, and Charles A. Nelson, of Nelson Associates; *World Affairs and the College Curriculum* by Richard N. Swift, of New York University; and a regional study on *International Relations in Institutions of Higher Education in the South* by Fred Cole, now of Washington and Lee University.

This final volume in the series is only incidentally a summary of the preceding volumes, although many of their conclusions and recommendations are restated in the following pages. Essentially, however, this volume returns to the theme of institutional policy, of administrative organization by which policy may be implemented, of the role—the responsibilities and limitations—of institutions of higher education in respect to world affairs. The second chapter of the volume deals with the responsibilities of liberal arts colleges for preparing citizens for a society in which international relations seem to have an overriding role. The following chapter reviews briefly the organizational structures for dealing with international matters which have been developed in a selected group of universities during four decades of experience and indicates the particular responsibilities and problems of universities. The fourth chapter describes the cultural activities of the Federal Government, as they have emerged to date, with which the nation's institutions of higher education should be related. It outlines an inventory of federal programs which have concern for higher education. The fifth chapter deals with the pervasive matter of interchange of students and scholars. And the concluding chapter again states briefly the issues which are before American academia—the issues on which each institution must determine a policy consistent with its own character and resources.

Related Studies on Higher Education and World Affairs

The Carnegie Endowment program, a pioneering enterprise whose reports have focused distinctively on policy and organization within institutions of higher education, is only one of a growing series of studies and publications in this field. Indeed, the studies in the Endowment series, including this final volume, draw very heavily upon a variety of studies and reports which have become quite characteristic of the literature on higher education during the last decade.

Grayson Kirk began the movement, in a sense, with his volume on *The Study of International Relations in American Colleges and Universities,* prepared for the Council on Foreign Relations just after the war.[7] This was followed in 1951 by a study by a Committee of the American Political Science Association, whose report on *Goals for Political Science* included considerable discussion of the relationship of international affairs to the curriculum in political science.[8] The Brookings Institution in a series of

[7] Grayson Kirk, *The Study of International Relations in American Colleges and Universities* (New York: Council on Foreign Relations, 1947), x + 113 pp.

[8] Committee for the Advancement of Teaching, American Political Science Association, *Goals for Political Science* (New York: William Sloane Associates, 1951), xxiv + 319 pp.

conferences and publications [9] promoted the analysis of issues of foreign policy in colleges and universities. The Social Science Research Council produced such studies as Charles Wagley's analysis of the rise of world-area studies in American universities [10] and Guy S. Metraux's early analysis of student interchange.[11] A volume published by the American Council on Education, reporting the deliberations of a major conference on universities and world affairs which was held at Estes Park in 1949, had widespread influence on American academic thinking.[12]

As the decade of the fifties advanced, an increasing number of studies by individual scholars, reports of committees and conferences, and descriptions of institutional developments appeared. The Foreign Language Association developed new programs and policies for language teaching. Papers and reports began to emerge from a newly created Association of Foreign Student Advisers. The Social Science Research Council sponsored a series of studies on foreign students from a number of countries,[13]

[9] Brookings Institution, Washington, D.C., annually from 1947 to 1952 published *Major Problems of United States Foreign Policy,* and ten times a year produced a supplement, *Current Developments in United States Foreign Policy.*

[10] Charles Wagley, *Area Research and Training: A Conference Report on the Study of World Areas,* Pamphlet 6 (New York: Social Science Research Council, June 1948), 58 pp.

[11] Guy S. Metraux, *Exchange of Persons: The Evolution of Cross-Cultural Education,* Pamphlet 9 (New York: Social Science Research Council, June 1952).

[12] Howard L. Nostrand and Francis J. Brown (eds.), *The Role of Colleges and Universities in International Understanding* (Washington, D.C.: American Council on Education, 1949), x + 137 pp.

[13] Among these studies, published by the University of Minnesota Press, are: Ralph L. Beals and Norman D. Humphrey, *No Frontier to Learning: The Mexican Student in the United States* (1957); John W. Bennett, Herbert Passin, and Robert K. McKnight, *In Search of Identity: The Japanese Overseas Scholar in America and Japan* (1958); Richard D. Lambert and Marvin Bressler, *Indian Students on an American Campus* (1956); Richard T. Morris, *The Two-Way Mirror, National Status in Foreign Students' Adjustment* (1960); Franklin D. Scott, *The American Experience of Swedish Students* (1955); and William H. Sewell and Oluf M. Davidson, *Scandinavian Students on an American Campus* (1961).

studies which contributed much to the volume by Cora Du Bois in the Carnegie Endowment Series. The annual census of foreign students published by the Institute of International Education gained significance and audience every year.

From Michigan State University came a series of studies supported by the Carnegie Corporation and directed by Edward W. Weidner. In this extensive program, launched in 1957, Mr. Weidner and a team of social scientists reviewed more than 380 programs operated in this country and abroad by 184 colleges and universities, and interviewed 2,000 persons connected with the projects. In *The World Role of Universities*,[14] Mr. Weidner summarizes all the findings and offers his interpretation and conclusions. A very useful feature of the volume is the author's bibliographical commentary covering the growing body of literature on the foreign relations of American universities.

An increasing number of documents appeared from the Government Printing Office, notably the report on *Government Programs in International Education*.[15] Percy Bidwell completed

[14] Edward W. Weidner, *The World Role of Universities* (New York: McGraw-Hill Book Co., 1962), 366 pp.

In the series, three volumes are published by the Institute of Research on Overseas Programs, which was established at Michigan State University (East Lansing) to administer the research grant. They are: Richard N. Adams and Charles C. Cumberland, *United States University Cooperation in Latin America* (1960); Bruce Lannes Smith, *Indonesian-American Cooperation in Higher Education* (1960); and Edward W. Weidner and associates, *The International Programs of American Universities* (1958). Published by the Michigan State University Press (East Lansing) are the following: John A. Garraty and Walter Adams, *From Main Street to the Left Bank* (1959); Walter Adams and John A. Garraty, *Is the World Our Campus?* (1960); and Henry Hart, *Campus India: An Appraisal of American College Programs in India* (1961). Published jointly by the Free Press (Glencoe, Ill.) and the Bureau of Social and Political Research of Michigan State University (East Lansing) is Martin Bronfenbrenner, *Academic Encounter: The American University in Japan and Korea* (1961).

[15] *Government Programs in International Education* (*A Survey and Handbook*), Forty-second Report by the Committee on Government Operations, House Report No. 2712, 85th Cong., 2d Sess., 1959 (Washington: Government Printing Office, 1959).

in 1962 a comprehensive study[16] on what American college students learn about world affairs, which will be discussed later.

All these studies, and others, are referred to in later pages of this volume. Of particular importance to the considerations here dealt with is a report published in 1960 bearing almost the same title as the exploratory study issued by the Carnegie Endowment in 1951. In 1960 a committee broadly representative of government, the major foundations, and American industry, working under the chairmanship of James L. Morrill, published the most comprehensive and significant statement which has yet appeared on American universities and world affairs.[17]

The present volume draws heavily upon these reports, as well as upon others recently published in its field. It focuses attention, however, not so much on government policies and problems in their relations with universities as on college and university policies and problems in their relations with government. American higher education, faced with serious problems of focus and of resources, of potentialities, responsibilities, and limitations, must, in its concerns with international affairs, put its house in order. This volume is hopefully a contribution to the

[16] Percy W. Bidwell, *Undergraduate Education in Foreign Affairs* (New York: Columbia University Press, 1962), 224 pp.

[17] The Committee on the University and World Affairs was composed of Harold Boeschenstein, president of Owens-Corning Fiberglas Corporation; Harvie Branscomb, chancellor of Vanderbilt University; Arthur S. Flemming, then Secretary of Health, Education, and Welfare; J. W. Fulbright, United States senator; John W. Gardner, president of the Carnegie Corporation; Franklin D. Murphy, chancellor of the University of California, Los Angeles; Philip D. Reed, formerly chairman of the board, General Electric Company; Dean Rusk, then president of the Rockefeller Foundation; and (chairman) J. L. Morrill, formerly president of the University of Minnesota. Its chief staff members were John B. Howard, Phillips Talbot, and Adam Yarmolinsky. Its report, issued early in 1961 under the title *The University and World Affairs,* deals with (1) The Educational Issue, (2) The American University as a Center of Learning and Service, (3) Educational Cooperation across National Boundaries, (4) Strengthening Our Educational Resources, and (5) Organizing for Educational Leadership. Copies were made available through the Ford Foundation, 477 Madison Avenue, New York 22, N.Y.; v + 84 pp.

appraisal of present academic operations, the assessment of our current failures and successes. It is designed to suggest policy bases for more effective academic adjustments to the continuing impact of world affairs on American higher education.

The Basic Concern of Higher Education with World Affairs

The question must continually be kept in mind, of course, why American higher education is being influenced and should be influenced by world affairs. "What in the world have world affairs to do with" higher education? The answer to the question lies not only in the characteristics of contemporary international relations, as indicated at the outset of this chapter, but also in the nature and distinctive qualities of colleges and universities themselves. The tradition of higher education reaches far back and has elements of permanence in its essential qualities. Higher education is not so much a handmaiden of politics as an inevitable partner in the international enterprise of the twentieth century.

Learning, the traditional and overarching concern of colleges and universities, is essential to the continuance of civilization. As the technological revolution continues its relentless course, the importance of learning, and of institutions of learning, to society is increasingly demonstrated. Learning, its constant advancement and endless preservation, is one of the values which international policies among governments must, in the long run, be designed to protect. And vital learning is requisite to the formulation of policy and to its execution. Institutions of higher education are established as centers of learning, with distinctive social responsibilities for advancing, preserving, and disseminating knowledge and that insight which is wisdom. They cannot discharge their responsibilities without defending the interests of learning on every frontier. Deterioration in international relations inevitably threatens learning. Colleges and universities perforce have a stake in the maintenance of the kind of peace which cherishes learning and the freedom of inquiry.

Learning, moreover, is universal in its nature. Scholarship advances as it is widely cultivated, as the contributions to knowledge from far places flow into one great stream, and as worldwide communication is easy and extensive. Barriers to the free flow of knowledge need to be kept at a minimum if the interests of learning are to be considered. Interchange of information is essential, as evidenced by the steady rise of international scholarly and professional associations and by the international documentary and translation services which modern society demands. If there were no international relations rising from other sources, colleges and universities would have to create their own international relations in the interest of the pursuit of learning to which they owe allegiance. It is in the interest of learning to keep as widely open as possible the international channels of communication.

The world is both a source of knowledge and a subject for increased study by modern colleges and universities. The programs of regional study which have arisen in recent decades, the flood of new languages scattered through our course offerings, professional studies in comparative law, public administration, and education alike attest the vital impact of world affairs on academic interests and also symbolize the responsibility of a college or university for widening the horizons for those whom it educates.

Ultimately, the nation's institutions of higher education are responsible for providing a considerable proportion of our youth with an education that is relevant to the moving issues of their age; and the interrelations of peoples, cultures, governments, and institutions on a shrinking globe have high priority among those issues. From the colleges and universities come the great preponderance of opinion makers in the population. The degree to which the college and university have widened their horizons, deepened their insights, and sharpened their judgments about the "endless web" of international contacts is the degree to which the university has contributed to the defense of learning and to the welfare of society. As was stated in the most recent Commission report on *The University and World Affairs:*

The greater concern of American universities with world affairs is but an appropriate educational response to matters of paramount concern to the individual American, to the nation and its new role, and to men everywhere. . . . These are matters not alone for the specialists. They are a dimension or whole new set of dimensions of the problems with which all American students and all American universities and colleges are or should be vitally concerned. In these new dimensions lie not only new public responsibilities and duties but exciting opportunities for the individual to be enriched as an educated man and citizen.[18]

[18] *Op. cit.*, p. 13.

2

College Education for Twentieth-Century Life

In his history of Harvard, Samuel Eliot Morison refers to the American college as "the despair of educational reformers and logical pedagogues, the astonishment of continental scholars, a place which is neither a house of learning nor a house of play, but a little of both; and withal a microcosm of the world in which we live."[1] The college is a unique American institution, whether it exists as a separate entity or as the undergraduate unit of a larger university. Its four years have a deep, nostalgic hold on American emotions. Once the privilege of a few, more than a third of the Americans graduating from high school now go on to a college of some character. The possession of a collegiate baccalaureate is now virtually prerequisite for higher posts not only in the professions and public life but also in all other areas of American business and industry.

Basically, the function of the college is to provide a liberal education, though inevitably career concerns creep into its curriculum, and in some cases it is directly vocational. It is built around a strange amalgam of concepts—the eighteenth-century gentleman, the citizen of a democracy, the devotee of learning, and the independent leader of a pragmatic society. At its best the college provides an education which transmits the traditions of culture as they are related to the vital forces of the learner's environment. For the individual student it provides a thoughtful

[1] Samuel Eliot Morison, *The Founding of Harvard College* (Cambridge, Mass.: Harvard University Press, 1935), p. 56.

balancing of concentration and distribution in his studies, ranging across the humanities and the natural and social sciences. To this formal curriculum of the worthy college is added what Cotton Mather described as "the collegiate way of life"—the microcosm of which Morison wrote and which Cardinal Newman praised. Curriculum and extracurriculum, under good circumstances, reinforce each other and merge into an educative experience of major value, a haunting combination of idealism and realism, of learning and of play, alike for older and younger members of the college community, as is indicated in the first volume of this series.[2]

While the traditions of the college, both on the campus and in the classroom, are strong and maintain a continuity in character and function for every institution, colleges inevitably reflect the social and intellectual changes going on within their supporting society. Indeed, the origins of change and development within a college lie largely outside it; the alert college reflects its society without simply bending before its transient breezes, and the college of the coming decade can be envisioned only by envisioning the United States of that decade. During the last century the curriculum has been remade by the forces of the scientific and technological revolution and the social movements related to the behavioral sciences. That remaking is still going on. The college of the present century, while continuing to adjust to scientific advance at an accelerating rate, is also beginning a basic and extensive reorientation to take cognizance of worldwide horizons, of the complex pattern of contemporary international relations, and of the particular role of the United States in world affairs.

It is, then, appropriate and even urgent, for the college to appraise itself in its relation to the moving forces of contemporary

[2] Howard E. Wilson, *American College Life as Education in World Outlook* (Washington: American Council on Education, 1956), xvii + 195 pp. The volume deals with the interrelations of campus and classroom, facilities for informal instruction about world affairs, student-faculty relations, student travel, and the general organization of a college community.

life, and among these forces international relations now have unprecedented importance. There are abundant indications that many of the issues in curriculum development, in student counseling, in educational finance and planning, in creating a campus community, are intimately related to the characteristics of international life. No college can afford to be unconcerned with such matters. The vitality of collegiate education for at least the remainder of this century is dependent to no small degree on the way in which it prepares students to face the realities of world affairs.

The College and International Affairs

What is it that the college should do for students as preparation for living in an era such as ours? What are the aspects of liberal education of greatest worth in the society of the coming generation? There can be no precise and easy answer to such questions, but the questions cannot be ignored. Even a preliminary and incomplete answer may suggest criteria for the appraisal of the college in contemporary society. It is, of course, not sufficient to say that the college student should be taught more about world affairs, important as this may be. The answer lies deeper—in the qualities of mind and outlook, of sensitivity and serenity which are requisite for the educated man in a democracy especially as he faces his responsibilities for national action on a world stage in a nuclear era. To determine these qualities, the values and processes of liberal education must be re-examined in relation to the international interests and responsibilities of the United States. The college graduate in American society must play a responsible role in the continuous debate on foreign policy, must vote for or against specific proposals of policy, must select the experts on whom to rely, and must live with the continuing problems of national security and of incomprehensibly total war. What can the college do to equip him for this role?

This question must ultimately be answered—in detail and

action—by every college for itself. But here at least certain illustrative aspects of an answer may be indicated. What are the characteristics most needed in modern man? One quality for the educated citizen is a sense of historical perspective, not only of the long sweep of history with its rise and fall of nations, but more specifically of the day-by-day motion of the historical stream. Not every incident is a crisis, though the vagaries of modern instantaneous communication sometimes make it seem so. There may be a certain calmness in a sense of history which is one mark of the educated man and which is particularly valuable in a somewhat trigger-happy age where a single mistake may engulf civilization. A sense of time, of what Charles Beard called the "seamless web" of human experience, is a valuable acquirement for modern man. What does the college do to develop it in all who are "liberally educated"?

A second acquirement, closely related to historical sensitivity, is insight into human nature, into the motives and aspirations and limitations of man. To what extent does the college student of today face the ancient query "What is man?" We look for answers, not only within the traditional theological framework, but also in the findings of contemporary psychology, psychiatry, medicine, and literature. Preliminary understanding of why we behave like human beings, and the means by which this behavior may be made constructive—or at least by which its worst excesses may be avoided—must be firmly embedded in the intellectual outlook of twentieth-century man. In understanding the drives of human behavior, individually and in mass, lies one requisite for the governance of men; and in this knowledge the citizens of a democracy must collectively outdistance the manipulative few of a monolithic society. To understand man is a universal need, made more urgent by today's capacity for self-destruction.

Third, the educated man of today needs a sense of the complexity of social action and the necessity of continuing adjustment to maintain a moving, virile equilibrium. Answers to most of the questions of international relations are not as definitive or as simple as we would often like them to be or as the extremists on either side assume them to be. Second thoughts are usually better than snap judgments, particularly where the fate of men and nations is involved. To what extent and by what means does the college develop a judicious-mindedness in its graduates? Without a strong tendency toward reflective analysis on complex issues, the modern citizen is too easily the victim of demagoguery. Yet, of course, the comprehension of this infinite complexity must not lead to despair or to drifting. It must result in patience and continued effort without abandonment of the values and aspirations which vitalize the lives of individuals and nations alike.

Fourth, and closely related to the development of perspective, to social sensitivity, to poised maturity, and to judicious habits of reflection, is facility in communication. This involves, under modern circumstances, effective communication in alien tongues, with culturally distant persons, and with the use of technical instruments and facilities previously unknown. The circumstances and qualities of life in modern America force more people to make more decisions about more matters of great consequence and with infinitely more rapidity than any past generation has ever had to do. This action of public policy-making and opinion-forming is closely related to the extraordinary technical expansion of communication facilities, and it involves clearer understanding and use of these facilities. But over and beyond this adjustment to technological phenomena is the linguistic—often the semantic—task by which educated men and women break the barriers of cultural isolation.

A fifth acquirement is scientific literacy, the ability to grasp at the nonscientist's level the nature and reach of science in its impact on security and welfare. Without basic insight into the nature and meaning of the scientific revolution, no man can be sufficiently liberally educated to cope with contemporary responsibilities. The study of science, not as a specialist devotee studies it, but in the manner in which the nonhistorian studies history, is central to the reform of liberal education in our times. It is a task few colleges, few scientists, and few curriculum makers have realistically faced. One cannot understand the world today without such an intellectual disciplining or participate as an educated citizen in the governance of our society without insight into the manner in which men, through science, have remade many controls of the physical world.

Perhaps the most important acquirement to be expected of the college graduate is a concept of the national purpose arising from our tradition, and of the general objectives to which American society is committed. A glimpse of the goals to be sought, of the values which are cherished, of the meaning of the good life toward which we aspire—without some such unifying and challenging concept made reasonably clear in the minds of its educated citizens, the vitality of the national effort is dissipated. The college experience which fails the student at this point does him major disservice. And, of course, this sense of the meaning of America is related to insight into the character of nationalism, to its force in history, to its limitations, to the relations among nations within a complex world. To see the United States as it has emerged, to know the image others have of it, to adhere strongly to the cluster of values which distinguishes it, is a part of the wisdom of citizens who can ensure the nation's future. This is a task not only of the study of history, including the history of science, but also of all other humanities and social sciences.

Such are the requisites, then, for educated men and women in the decades immediately ahead. Development of these qualities should be the constant and underlying concern of the nation's colleges. Unless these institutions can cultivate in students a sense of historical perspective, insight into human nature and behavior, a sense of continuing adjustment to changing complexities, a high facility in communication, insight into the scientific forces which influence current society, insight into the forces of nationalism and international action, and a clearer concept of the underlying national purpose and its priority values, the four years of college life will not have been as liberating as this era requires.

There is, of course, nothing sacrosanct about this formulation of the personal acquirements made important by the interrelations of liberal education and contemporary society; the points may be expressed in various ways, and this list of seven is assuredly only a beginning. But the point of view which leads us to such a list—that liberal education can be defined only in terms of personal qualities needed for intelligent participation in the society of an era—is of first importance. Only as those who shape the character of the American college concern themselves assiduously with this matter will the goals of liberal education be reached and ultimately be effective.

Studies of American Colleges and International Relations

The literature on the American college, which has expanded voluminously during recent decades, contains numerous proposals and reports on special programs or projects by which colleges have sought to adjust the elements of liberal education to the characteristics of an international era. Many of these have been referred to in earlier volumes of this series, particularly in Richard Swift's analysis of the college curriculum.[3] In this seventh volume of the Carnegie Endowment Studies in Universities and World Affairs, Swift presents a searching discussion of the multiple meanings of "world affairs," their relationship to the liberal arts in general and to the humanities, history, the social

[3] Richard N. Swift, *World Affairs and the College Curriculum* (Washington: American Council on Education, 1959), ix + 144 pp.

sciences, the natural sciences, and mathematics in particular, and the problems posed by undergraduate courses and majors in the field. He thinks that the conventional introductory course in international relations is not best suited for the general student and urges that the colleges take an interdisciplinary approach in teaching about world affairs. He also points out the need for more effective language teaching, for the study of the cultures of Asia and Africa, and for higher standards of secondary education as a basis for college and university work.

Another study concerned with general undergraduate education in foreign affairs is Percy Bidwell's volume which appeared in 1962.[4] Bidwell's conclusions and recommendations are based on interviews and correspondence with several hundred teachers and administrators and on examination of enrollments in courses dealing specifically with international affairs. Enrollment in such courses was low, and very few nonspecialist students in international relations were among the enrollees. Bidwell suggests that more could be done to increase enrollments in these courses, primarily through guidance and perhaps through the waiving of prerequisites in some cases.

To get some measure of the typical undergraduate's knowledge of foreign affairs, an 80-question test, prepared by the Educational Testing Service, was given in the spring of 1960 to 1,958 students selected at random from the senior classes at 175 colleges and universities. As is so frequently the case in tests given to a sampling of students, the results were depressing. On the average, students answered correctly only 55 percent of the questions—44 out of 80. No doubt the examination was competently and validly designed, but it is possible that nonspecialist seniors, embroiled in all the distractions of the last weeks of their undergraduate experience, might have misinterpreted some of the intricate items in the test. It is to be noted, too, that the test was not

[4] Percy W. Bidwell, *Undergraduate Education in Foreign Affairs* (New York: Columbia University Press, 1962).

given at a number of institutions known for their curricular and extracurricular emphases on international relations. The use of this test, while revealing and properly disturbing, is basically an evidence of the need for further experimentation with the means of testing in this field.

Bidwell found that most American history courses, in which large numbers of students are typically enrolled, were taught from a relatively parochial point of view; courses in European history gave better "foreign exposure" but enrolled fewer students. He found little or no international content in the introductory courses in economics, sociology, and anthropology. The beginning courses in political science concentrated largely on American national government. Courses in geography he found almost nonexistent so far as student enrollments were concerned. He felt that the courses in Western civilization, although often superficial, probably contributed more than any other lower-division courses to the nonspecialist students' understanding of at least part of the international scene.

Bidwell recommends that in most colleges and universities the introductory courses in American history and the social sciences be reorganized so as to impart more knowledge of the history, the political institutions, and the economic and social conditions of other countries. The comparisons and contrasts that such revision would require would also deepen the students' understanding of American institutions and policies.

To exploit the rich contributions that modern literature and languages can make to the knowledge of foreign countries, he points out that teachers will require more training than they now receive in cultural anthropology and sociology. Courses in Western civilization are already overloaded with material, and Bidwell suggests that they be supplemented with one or more courses giving concentrated attention to a non-Western area or that they be replaced with courses in world history and geography.

Many developments in widely scattered American colleges

illustrate both the possibilities and problems of the changes we are now going through. Oberlin College, for example, has long cultivated an interest in world affairs among its students, as much by extracurricular as by curricular means, which has led many of its graduates into foreign service. Many of the religiously oriented colleges have systematically contributed to the numbers of foreign missionaries who have long represented one of the major cultural ties of the United States with other areas of the world. Carleton College, after the establishment there of the Frank B. Kellogg Foundation, developed a special sequence of courses on international affairs as a part of liberal education and arranged a major program of general lectures and forums giving particular attention to international matters. Immediately after World War II, Colgate University entered into a comprehensive curriculum reform designed to apply at the undergraduate level some of the concepts that were being developed at the graduate level in a variety of world-area study centers. Students concentrated on one of several areas in their humanities and social science courses during the sophomore year and attended periodic general lectures on issues common to the various areas. In the senior year, Colgate developed an unusual course on American values as related to world movements—a curriculum innovation of very great potential not only for its world focus, but also as a synthesizing influence at the end of liberal education. Dartmouth's long-developed course on Great Issues served a similar function.

During the early 1950's the faculty at San Francisco State College [5] developed with great travail a two-year sequence of general education in the social sciences which was climaxed by a semester devoted to world affairs. The semester's instruction departed from the customary focus on political science, and approached world affairs through the analysis of cultural contacts

[5] Charles A. McClelland, *College Teaching of International Relations: Problems of Organization and Collaboration* (San Francisco, Calif.: Department of International Relations, San Francisco State College, 1962), xi + 382 pp.

as seen primarily through sociology and anthropology. A considerable emphasis on international matters appears in many of the general introductory courses or sequences in the social sciences. College programs in business administration include increasing material on the world economy and international trade; education majors are increasingly likely to study comparative education.

A number of colleges have developed programs for relatively systematic incorporation of student travel or residence abroad as a planned part of liberal education. The Junior Year Abroad plan survived the exigencies of World War II, and has grown substantially in recent years. Through cooperative support, or by the action of individual colleges or universities, centers for study for American students are located throughout Europe and in parts of Asia. These are resident centers, pioneered by the University of Maryland and Sweet Briar College, offering instruction with the cooperation of foreign universities under arrangements making the transfer of credits easily feasible. By the late 1950's many colleges and universities had established off-campus centers in foreign areas for both undergraduate and graduate students.

The incorporation of foreign experience into the liberal arts program of American colleges is by no means dependent entirely on such foreign centers, operating either as separate entities to provide a year's study abroad, or as planned parts of a four-year sequence. Arrangements for summer study abroad or educational travel with academic interest have become commonplace since World War II. The University of Minnesota developed one of the early programs of academic value, sending selected students for a summer of field observation after preparation throughout the preceding academic year. Students prepare papers on the basis of their summer observations and are able to secure regular academic credit for such work.[6] A considerable number of institutions developed similar programs for language students.

[6] For this and other summer study programs, see Wilson, *op. cit.*, pp. 141–65.

Sometimes summer study tours are too nearly the hobby and exclusive concern of travel-minded faculty members, but in other cases the periods of summer travel-study are carefully integrated into the four-year liberal arts experience. Western College for Women in Oxford, Ohio, for example, schedules a world-area trip for selected students during the summer between their junior and senior years. Much of the junior year is devoted to courses focused on the chosen area, including language study; the senior year includes both curricular and extracurricular utilization of the summer experiences. Close contact with alumnae of Western College living in the travel area is maintained and adds substantially to the cultural reality of the travel and the international interests of the campus itself.

A major factor in the development of insight into other cultures and international relations for American students is their contact with students from other countries studying in the United States. Much has been written about the reception, counseling, and training of foreign students, but too little has as yet appeared on the effect their presence has or may have in the education of American youth. Virtually every institution of higher education in the United States now receives foreign students. The relationships between foreign and American students vary greatly from campus to campus, and even more from personality to personality. Studies repeatedly reveal that foreign students wish to know American students better than they do, and particularly that they want to tell American students more about their own background. Wherever close friendships develop between American and foreign students as individuals, these friendships are extremely effective in the education of both. Whatever the college can do to promote such friendships among well-balanced students is a contribution to liberal education as well as to international understanding. In more general terms, the international clubs and the festivals and other student events which appear regularly in the calendars of many campuses are worthy contributions to an international outlook.

Organization and Administration of College Interests in International Relations

Perhaps enough has been said to suggest something of the variety of ways in which colleges in the United States have sought to strengthen the international element in their programs of liberal education, extending from the introduction of new course sequences and the modification of content in existing courses to the development of cocurricular programs and emphasis on social and recreational enterprises. The difficulty is that few colleges, if any, have developed an imaginative, creative, over-all coordination of the segments of education for international realities which have already come into being. Special enterprises abound, but the constructive imagination which went into the remaking of American college life in the 1930's or again during the first decade after World War II seems to have evaporated. What is needed today is a clearer perception of the total impact of world affairs in the American college and an effectively coordinated, comprehensive program for dealing with its problems and potentials.

The basic need in most colleges is comprehensive, thoughtfully determined policy—a continuing analysis of the role of the college in international matters and of the role of international matters in liberal education. For each institution something like a master plan, creatively conceived and flexible, is needed both as a framework for academic operations and as a set of criteria against which to evaluate further innovations. Without an adequately conceived policy, wastage of efforts and neglect of opportunities are almost certain to result.

No single element in a college structure can provide the necessary coordination. The office of the president must be sympathetically involved, but the kind of over-all policy and program which is desired cannot be produced by central administration alone. Specialists in international relations cannot speak for the whole college even though their voices are essential in the discussion. The foreign student adviser, whether a part-time faculty member or on the staff of the dean of students, cannot alone determine college policy even on student affairs. Faculty members in a variety of fields, personally and emotionally animated by concern with foreign and international matters, cannot alone lift the curriculum and their colleagues to the level of wisdom needed. A combination of these administrative and faculty voices, together with those of student leaders, must engage in the analysis and determination of policy for an over-all college program.

The typical college needs a consultative, coordinating, policy-making committee representing all the groups within the campus community which are concerned with the international facets of liberal education. This committee must have ready access to the president and deans, must have academic prestige among the faculty, and must be recognized by students as an alert and creative group. Its functions ought not to be administrative; rather, through suggestion, consultation, and review, it should encourage action by those who shape both the curriculum and the cocurriculum. Such a committee should engage in an informal and continuing inventory of resources, programs, possibilities, and problems bearing on the interrelations between liberal education and international education.

Questions a College Should Consider

If such a committee were established, and charged with the task of discerning the range of desirable adjustments requisite for reorienting liberal education to the international concerns of our age, it would perforce deal with a range of pertinent issues. It may be useful, therefore, to suggest here some of the questions such a committee should explore and, in so doing, revise in the light of a decade of experience the exploratory questions raised in the Carnegie Endowment's publication on *Universities and World Affairs* in 1951. The questions briefly discussed in the following pages are not listed in order of importance, or as a definitive battery. They do, however, summarize some of the main concerns expressed in recent years by individuals and committees and organizations active in the adjustment of liberal education to twentieth-century civilization. Taken together, they envisage the kind of over-all coordinated program the liberal arts college should today be seeking. They are the kinds of interrelated questions with which responsible faculty and administrative agencies and student leaders in every college should be wrestling.

1. *Are all students who graduate from college given instruction on the nature of American society and the sources and directions of the nation's foreign policy?* International relations begin with nations, and the first element in wisdom about international affairs is deep understanding of one's own nation—its traditions, its resources and limitations, its continuing policies, its problems, and its prestige. This instruction may be given in any of a variety of courses ranging through the social sciences and the humanities; the important matter is that the Socratic injunction "know thyself" should be applied to the nation-state by its educated citizens. To this end it is also important that we know how others see us; it is essential to view national policies in terms of feasible alternatives, and it is paramount that national values and ideals be comprehended as something more worthy and enduring than slogans and shibboleths. In any college it is not sufficient simply that courses covering this area be offered; they or selected portions of them must be incorporated as *requisite* in the liberal arts program. The goal which Colgate sought in its senior course on American values in world society is one with which all colleges should be concerned. Sometimes the goal can be obtained by a course on diplomatic history, or on the American tradition,

or on the sociological structure of American life. Sometimes, as at St. John's, a series of required, extraclass lectures may serve this end. The college, however, should not rest easy until some form of such instruction, of the highest vitality, is provided for all students who receive the award of its baccalaureate.

2. *Are students made familiar, at the value level, with a culture in addition to their own?* Few experiences are of greater consequence in liberal education than that of becoming sufficiently familiar with another culture to understand its value system and to be able to see the patterns of behavior which emerge from that value system. At this level the student can "put himself in another's place" without losing allegiance to his own code of action and ideals. On occasion this insight may be provided by instruction in literature or by language study which is focused on cultural analysis. The experience may be gained through cultural anthropology or social psychology or history. Combinations of elements from all these fields organized as area studies within the liberal arts curriculum are possible. In such a program, music and the arts have special value. But a superficial study of another country, a glossing over of national differences or likenesses, a sentimental friendliness for another society will not suffice. To experience another culture is a strenuous intellectual exercise calling for the greatest sensitivity. But it is an essential step toward the wisdom requisite for educated men and women in any age, and vitally important in an era such as ours.

3. *Do students master a language in addition to English?* The entire American educational system is, in this decade, reviewing its approach to the teaching of foreign languages. Developments within the elementary and secondary schools are likely to provide coming college generations with greater facility in the use of a second language, but even under present circumstances the liberal arts college may do much more in the way of language instruction than is now ordinarily done. Insight into another culture based upon familiarity with its language has traditionally

been an aspect of liberal education, leading, at its best, to what the Harvard Report on *General Education in a Free Society* called "a Copernican step, one of the most liberating, the most exciting, and the most sobering opportunities for reflection that the humanities can offer." [7] An excellent summary of the situation and prospects in the United States for language teaching is given in the earlier volume in this series by Richard Swift.[8] The report of the Morrill Committee, published in 1961, refers to "the crucial inadequacy of over-all American competence in foreign languages" and urges strenuous improvement in this field both for humanistic and for highly practical reasons.[9]

The teaching of language is more than the offering of a variety of courses. Basic to mastery of a language is a sufficient sequence of courses to pass beyond the initial obstacles of grammar and vocabulary and reach a level of cultural insight. To satisfy the language requirement in liberal education by two one-year courses in different languages is an absurdity; and, for the student, the failure to master one language and the dispersal of effort over more than one language without mastery is a waste of valuable time. The needs of our era demand as perhaps never before language competency rather than units of credit. Within a college, only the languages for which expert instruction can be provided should be taught, but it is greatly to be hoped that, throughout the nation, the languages critical to international relations can be taught to very large numbers of college students and that the variety of lesser languages brought into our cultural ken by contemporary life can be acquired—but acquired well—by smaller groups of students. The national need is for competency by some college graduates in a wide range of languages

[7] *General Education in a Free Society: Report of the Harvard Committee* (Cambridge, Mass.: Harvard University Press, 1945), p. 120.

[8] *Op. cit.*, pp. 47–55.

[9] *The University and World Affairs* (New York: Ford Foundation, 1961), pp. 25–27.

and competence by most of the educated group in a second major language.

4. *Do all students gain insight into the nature and social significance of the scientific and technological revolution?* This is an age of science in which scientific technology is particularly crucial to national security and the balance of political power as well as to industrial development and the whole complex of health, education, and welfare. During the last century the study of science has moved from the periphery to the center of the liberal arts curriculum. Virtually every college in the country is already concerned with laying the scientific foundations of an education for emerging scientists. The last five years have witnessed an enormously increased concern among colleges in the training of young scientists and this has profoundly affected the total curriculum of the colleges.

Yet relatively few colleges have dealt adequately with the equally important tasks of increasing the social understanding of young scientists and of increasing the scientific insight of non-scientists. The essential assumptions of science and the social significance of both pure and applied science are requisite concerns for the educated men and women of this century, whatever their scholarly specializations or vocations. Whether this concern is expressed in a variety of courses or in a general sequence on the nature of science, as was done at Chicago, it must be made clear to all students. As has been said, without some knowledge in this area, at least enough to exercise judgment in selecting the experts on whom one relies, no citizen can discharge his responsibility in the continuing public debate on such questions as the testing of nuclear weapons, the control of armaments, the extension of public health, or the interrelationships of economic development and technical education.

5. *Does the college program adequately introduce students to the non-Western as well as to the Western World?* As was stressed in chapter 1 of this volume, the wide variety of cultures involved

in the international conversation today, with their diverse values and assumptions and goals, is one cause of the confusion of the times. The traditional liberal arts curriculum circumscribed by the confines of Western civilization is no longer adequate to provide the educated man anywhere in the world with the insights needed for his role in modern society.

Within the college curriculum, the extension of the history program to include the rich traditions of Asia and Africa, as well as Western Europe and the Americas, is already generally well under way. Whether this is done through a single survey course or through a variety of regional courses or by other ways is not so important as is the need for requiring basic instruction on the non-Western World as a part of the program for all college students. The same is true in the study of world literature. It is requisite that all college graduates have some acquaintance with the classics of the Orient as well as of the Occident and with the interrelation of movements in literature and the arts and scholarship among a wide range of cultures. In the arts—music, painting, sculpture, ceramics, theater, handicrafts—lie rich opportunities for extending the cultural horizons of students.

It is obvious that a college curriculum which draws its content from all the major cultures of the globe will not be put together simply by adding new courses as horizons are extended. What is needed is a fundamental reanalysis of the basic fields of which the curriculum is composed, particularly in the humanities and social sciences. An artful reweaving of the tapestries of history, literature, linguistics, and the fine arts, with a view to resynchronizing the liberal arts curriculum with the character and resources of modern culture is demanded. It is quite possible that, if this reweaving can be creatively achieved, the need for an elective system in college programs will be substantially reduced.

6. *Do students acquire insight into the nature of nation-states, of the relationships among modern states, and of the international agencies now in operation?* It is a part of education for national

citizenship in its twentieth-century context that college students should study in systematic fashion the nature of modern states and the techniques of international action among them. The study of international relations has come into the college curriculum in recent decades; a summary of the trends and issues in such teaching is found in the volume in this series by Richard Swift already referred to.[10]

It is fairly common for a college to offer a course in international relations, but far less common for it to be taken by any appreciable number of students, even by students majoring in the field of political science. Though international relations is sometimes taught by an available faculty member without special training in the field, there is a steady trend toward better instruction by qualified specialists. Certainly, the point has now been reached at which one or more specialists in international relations is requisite to every adequately balanced liberal arts faculty. The problem of fitting this instruction into the basic curriculum pattern of most institutions, however, has not yet been solved. An interdisciplinary approach to such a course, involving a combination of political science, economics, and sociology may be one means of widening registration in some institutions. Inclusion of international relations in a general introductory course in the social sciences is another approach. However, an over-all reappraisal of the patterns of requirements among courses with an objective emphasis on requiring the courses of greatest relevance to a functional liberal education will be necessary.

7. *Does the college provide a high-level forum for the presentation of current international issues and for student discussion of world affairs?* As has been stressed, not all of liberal education is provided in the formal curriculum; the collegiate way of living has its influence and potential also. Students may be alerted and informed on many aspects of international relations through a well-developed cocurricular program.

[10] *Op. cit.*, pp. 96–155.

In some colleges, Haverford College, for instance, distinguished leaders of public and international affairs are invited on occasion as guests of the college for a few days. They lecture to the college assembly, dine with student leaders, and engage in discussion sessions. In other colleges, series of general lectures often closely related to course sequences, as at St. John's and at Colgate, bring students and faculty together in a forum situation. A well-planned program in the College Union ordinarily provides something equivalent to the Union debates at Oxford. Student clubs devoted to international relations often provide a continuing opportunity for informal lecture-discussion situations. In passing it should be noted that opportunities for faculty members to engage, through forums and club discussions, in the analysis of contemporary events are ordinarily advantageous both for curriculum improvement and the intellectual upgrading of college life.

It is important that those concerned with fitting liberal education to twentieth-century demands utilize carefully all the potentialities in the cocurricular approach. It is particularly desirable that the college administration, the faculty, and student leaders join in the task of creating an intellectually creative campus environment. Opportunities for free discussion of international questions are a vital part of any community which cherishes academic freedom and are conducive to the sense of responsibility which makes that freedom viable.

8. *Is there a conscious and planned policy for utilizing foreign students on the campus as a resource for educating American students?* This chapter has earlier mentioned the potential of foreign students as a resource in liberal education. The potential is released through policies concerning housing of foreign students, policies by which they may share in student government and club activities, counseling programs, and through the services of a foreign student adviser. Sometimes in connection with student clubs and sometimes in more formal class situations,

foreign students may serve effectively as teachers. They may be assistants in language courses and contributors to the arts and humanities program. Through exhibits and special performances, they may contribute to the understanding of their own culture.

But the effective element is their friendly interrelationship with the general student body, not as lionized attractions but as persons. If Americans and foreign students are in any way segregated in the college dining halls or in the student union—if foreign students associate primarily among themselves on the campus or in the town—the visitors lose a commonly desired identification with their hosts, and the hosts lose an opportunity for deeper insight into other cultures.

9. *Is there a planned program for incorporating American student travel or residence abroad within the liberal arts program?* It has been already pointed out that an increasing number of colleges are sponsoring study tours for students, related closely to the pattern of courses offered; the junior year abroad is now a standard operation; Stanford, Syracuse, the University of California, and other institutions now maintain "branch campuses" abroad. Some of these enterprises may be on occasion academically inadequate, but their standards have risen steadily in recent years and there is every indication that they will become increasingly a part of the American enterprise in education.

10. *Does the college encourage foreign travel and study by faculty members, and does it bring visiting professors from abroad systematically to the campus?* The background, experience, and insight of individual faculty members is what makes any course or curriculum come alive. A provincial-minded faculty is not one which will widen the horizons of students. Under present conditions in the United States opportunity for faculty members to travel, to study or undertake research abroad, to participate in international cultural activities is greater than ever before. Yet these opportunities, used at the personal initiative of faculty members, are rarely utilized on a long-range basis as a

means of increasing the potency of the faculty as a whole. Only a few colleges have developed a long-range plan for providing all faculty members with foreign experience as a means of improving the college. Very few institutions have a long-range plan of Fulbright applications, for example, as a means of curriculum enrichment. Plans for sabbatical leaves are common, but less common are the administrative arrangements by which faculty members can go on leave to participate in government or foundation enterprises abroad without loss of retirement and sabbatical benefits and promotion opportunities. Each college needs to do whatever it can to facilitate faculty participation in overseas experience as a means of faculty growth. It is often feasible for a college to place faculty members on foreign assignment in connection with government AID contracts, even though these contracts are ordinarily with universities.

These ten questions have focused on the qualities of liberal education which seem to have particular relevance to contemporary life. But, as was indicated earlier, the college is in many cases somewhat vocational in its emphasis. For this reason an eleventh question should be added:

11. *Do the vocational programs of the college alert students to the international realities of their career areas?* If the college conducts a teacher education program, it cannot afford to ignore the current renaissance in comparative education. Students in business need an understanding of world economic geography and of the nature of international trade. It is very often in such courses, practical in the sense of their orientation toward careers, that students' interest in world affairs is aroused; such courses may, in many cases, make the more general concerns of liberal education come alive for many college students.

It is to such questions as these—dealing with the curricular and cocurricular approaches to a deeper understanding of our own national characteristics and testing, to deeper insight into the values of another culture, to facility in language and the techniques of communication, to a layman's grasp of the social significance of science, to the contrasts of Western and non-Western cultures, to an understanding of the nature of modern states and their complex interrelations, to the continuing analysis of current issues, to the use of foreign students and of student travel as educative resources, to the building of a college faculty experienced in foreign cultures and world affairs, and to the relation of world affairs to student career interests—that a college administration and faculty, in current years, must give urgent thought. These are among the questions on which long-range decisions must be made if the basic relationship between education and society within an internationally responsible United States is to continue healthy.

Needed: A Comprehensive College Policy

It is, of course, not adequate to deal with such questions as these in separation from each other. Comprehensive analysis and planning, with a program as wide as a functional liberal education is wide, must be the goal. And, as has been said, even the machinery for such continuing analysis and comprehensive planning in most colleges is today nonexistent or inadequate. The president's office, as the central administration of the college, is critical to the success or failure of both the comprehensive planning and the individual items of the program, but the college presidency is almost inevitably so beset with immediate problems that thoughtful, long-range, deeply experimental, and comprehensive planning is neglected. The tendency is to proceed with fragments of adjustments which are immediately practical and to hope ultimately to coalesce them into a defensible whole. Some gains are made by such a procedure, but the coalescence of fragments is rarely attained. The kind of creative thinking about the liberal arts college which, within another framework of concerns, produced not so long ago the experimental programs of Reed, Sarah Lawrence, Bennington, Rollins, the Harvard House plan, and the Swarthmore program seems strangely and disturbingly nonexistent today. It is a part of the unfinished business of the managers of liberal education to analyze the full impact of cultural and humane interests within world affairs and to face the requisite adjustments in program creatively and experimentally.

In guiding this pervasive and basic readjustment, the influence of certain factors is already clear. The experience we have had to date in adjusting the college to the impact of world affairs has amply demonstrated that it is the business of the college to educate, not to carry out sentimental or propagandistic or shortsightedly political programs which have momentary popularity. It seems also clear that the basic analysis and adjustment which is needed must extend over the whole range of the curriculum and the extracurriculum—that the first needs closer relation to contemporary realities and the second needs greater consciousness of the depth and background of current events and interests. It is clear, too, that the recognition of science as central to liberal thought and the contemporary effectiveness of educated men cannot be ignored. It is also evident that the mobility of students in a world potent with educative experience is something which should be recognized within the academic framework.

To emphasize an intellectual and experimental approach to education for international affairs is not, of course, to ignore the importance of a deeply moral element and sensitive, responsible purpose in the liberal education which is appropriate for the decades that are ahead. It is highly important that the liberal arts college help increasing numbers of its students to capture the sense of dedication and experience of service to the general welfare which some students earlier expressed in various forms of missionary activity. The college graduates, for example, who once taught for a time in an institution like Robert College in Istanbul often gained the capstone of liberal education by that experience. The summer work camps of the American Friends and other groups—and now the Peace Corps—provide a useful and deeply moral experience. Service experience may deepen the insights, widen the horizons, and focus the idealism of young men and women, particularly if it is shaped in an intellectual framework.

The Peace Corps programs now established as one element in American foreign policy are a unique challenge to liberal education. For many able and responsible students, adequately trained for the tasks they undertake, a tour of duty in the Peace Corps may give richer meaning to life, may help interrelate idealism and realism, may provide the satisfactions of service and direct participation in human and humane affairs. But the possibilities in the Peace Corps program will be best achieved if participation in the program is not an idle or extraneous choice by students, but is a planned climax to a liberal education and perhaps a preliminary internship related to graduate studies. If the Peace Corps continues as an instrument of American foreign policy, it should be able to recruit young people who have consciously been in preparation for it through their college years. More thoughtful articulation between college and such internships in reality as the Peace Corps provides is desirable and feasible, as will be discussed later in this volume.

All of the lines of development by which the liberal arts college may fit itself more vitally into American needs during the closing decades of the twentieth century require structural innovations and administrative realignments within the colleges. Sensitive sympathy and aid are required from the central administration. A wider institutional involvement is also requisite, an involvement of more than the personal enthusiasms of a few faculty and students. As has been suggested, a carefully established committee, representative of the responsible centers and scholarly fields on the campus, to deal with policies and proposals and to be continually alert to this particular interest, is desirable. Ordinarily such a committee functions more adequately if it has a secretariat in the form of a continuing administrative office devoted to the interrelations of academic and international matters. It seems likely that an increasing number of colleges will find this arrangement useful as a means of coordinating curriculum changes, of selecting and receiving foreign students, of providing faculty opportunities for study and work abroad, of encouraging student travel for study purposes, of planning extracurriculum developments, of discerning the colleges' responsibilities in adult education about world affairs, and of sustaining the growing relationships with government and foundations on international matters. The deepest concern of such a committee, of course, is the development of institutional policy—a policy and plan for keeping liberal education attuned to the significant influences in American life for the proximate future.

3

American Universities and World Affairs

THE LARGER AND more comprehensive units in American higher education which we loosely call universities have even more extensive and clear-cut responsibilities under the impact of contemporary world affairs than have American colleges. The undergraduate programs of the universities are faced with the same problems and potentials that the separate colleges are, with, very often, added complexities as well as advantages derived from their immediate relationship to graduate and professional schools. The graduate schools themselves, both academic and professional, are involved in the training of specialists in international relations and regional or area studies; in research covering a wide front from linguistics to nuclear physics and the laws of space; and in direct participation in governmental and intergovernmental programs through lending of personnel, contracts for services and training, leadership in adult continuing education, and regular consultation with agencies having political responsibility.

Even more than the colleges, the universities are caught up in a network of international relations based on scholarly and professional concerns. The universities are involved, not only through increased specialization in wide-ranging intellectual and esthetic interests, but also through international associations of scholars and professional specialists, and through a growing network of organized institutional contacts. Universities today, public or private, are closely related to government, and government increasingly involves universities in its operations. In no area is this relationship more apparent and more pervasive than in international concerns.

The involvement of universities in foreign policy and international relations has come about with great rapidity, particularly in the four decades since World War I. Like the colleges, universities have often adjusted to international interests in piecemeal fashion, accepting students from abroad, developing the new fields of scholarship in international relations and in area study, contracting with government for research and training programs at home and for services abroad, and expanding programs in some areas even at the expense of others. The desirable degree of coordination of activities within any university has not yet been attained—or even ascertained. Exactly as the departments and agencies of the Federal Government have been groping for the most effective pattern for national activities in international cultural relations in recent years, universities have, largely by trial and error, been moving toward a more effective organization and structure for dealing with the impacts and responsibilities of foreign policy and world affairs.

In order to discern the patterns of organization by which universities have sought to carry out their responsibilities and at the same time sought to safeguard their unique institutional academic character, it will be worthwhile to look briefly at the experience of a number of universities over recent decades. The trend of university developments, so far as pattern and organization are concerned, may be revealed in the accounts of a representative group of American institutions which have, in their own ways, come to grips with world affairs during the years since World War I. For this purpose, and in roughly chronological order, case study résumés of developments at Denver, Chicago, Stanford, Columbia, Harvard, Michigan State, and the University of California, Los Angeles, may be examined. In the experiences of these institutions are reflected some of the major directions of growth in university adjustments to international developments. They may illustrate in concrete terms the range of possibilities and problems which is characteristic of all of higher education during these decades.

The University of Denver

One of the early developments in university programs in international relations appeared at the University of Denver. At the suggestion of Chancellor Heber Harper, in 1923, a Denver businessman, James H. Causey, established the Social Science Foundation, with property amounting to approximately $1.3 million. The foundation [1] was given to the University of Denver but was established as an autonomous entity with its own Board of Directors, on which the university administration and trustees were represented. From the outset, the foundation was deeply concerned with international matters, though it used the term in a much broader sense than concern only with the relations among governments. Its trustees felt that international relations

> really include the relations of peoples in their many forms of group life, such as the impact of religions, educational systems, economic and industrial organizations, as well as governments. How these forms of life may be organized within and related to each other so as to make for peace and fullness of life for all mankind would represent the broad outline of the field of study of the Foundation.[2]

Under its first director, Ben Cherrington, who served for twenty-five years, and his successors Elizabeth Fackt, Dale Fuller, and Joseph Korbel, the foundation developed unusual programs of international study for the university, the Denver community, and the entire Rocky Mountain area. It pioneered

[1] See Morrison Shafroth, *The Social Science Foundation of the University of Denver* (Denver, Colo.: University of Denver, n.d.), iv + 13 pp. See also the pamphlet of the same title issued in 1954. The author, however, is indebted chiefly to Dr. Cherrington and later directors of the foundation for personal conversations and correspondence on which this account is based.

[2] Minutes of the Board of Trustees, Social Science Foundation, June 23, 1927.

in the adult education appropriate for a university by sponsoring round tables, study seminars, community lectures, and radio and television programs. It was also a unit within the university and quickly took form as the university's Department of International Relations. In that capacity, it created an academic pattern and program which should be examined as a pioneering effort in the adjustment of American universities to the pressures and potentialities of twentieth-century life.

The Department of International Relations, independently financed and directed through the foundation, employed a staff of faculty rank which offered courses in international relations and both stimulated and served the international interests of other departments within the university's Division of Social Sciences. Courses concerned with aspects of international relations were offered from time to time in history, psychology, sociology, anthropology, and economics as well as in political science. A pioneering undergraduate course in international relations was established as a part of the program in liberal education, and an advanced seminar in the same field widened the international insights of graduate students in the social sciences. An undergraduate major in international relations was supervised not only by the foundation staff, but by a committee representing other departments in the social sciences and humanities.

Not only did the department concern itself with an instructional program, it also supported research studies, many of which required periods of study abroad; these travel aids, ordinarily made available for faculty members, preceded and heralded certain aspects of the Fulbright program. Even more extensively, the foundation concerned itself with the foreign students who were arriving in increasing numbers. It developed counseling services for them, stimulated community reception of them, aided financially those in urgent need, and mobilized the foreign students as an educational influence in the life of the campus. The foundation supported and guided student clubs devoted to international interests and systematically enriched the cultural and intellectual life of the university by bringing outstanding speakers on world affairs to the campus. Through its director and other staff members, it served the government in a variety of ways; it was the director, on leave from the University of Denver, who established the first office of cultural relations in the Department of State in 1938.

The Denver Department of International Relations, then, brought into one center of academic responsibility instruction on international relations, stimulation and service to the international aspects of all the social sciences and humanities, general supervision of foreign students, research and related travel abroad, the university's work in adult and community education, and the utilization of extracurricular activities as influences in the development of an international outlook. This combination of functions worked well for the University of Denver. It was particularly effective in relating foreign students to the instructional program and in interrelating the academic program to far-flung activities of adult education in the Rocky Mountain area.

In recent years, decline in value of the holdings of the Social Science Foundation has curtailed many of the activities of the Department of International Relations. The heavy commitments in adult education over the Rocky Mountain area have had to be reduced, and the foundation has turned to an emphasis on the production of research studies. More recently, gifts to Denver from the Ford Foundation are making possible the redevelopment of the earlier extensive program, and may certainly result in integrating the foundation more closely within the university. But whatever form the developments at Denver take during the 1960's, the earlier years of work there are a significant part of the historical record of American academic restructuring under the impact of international concerns.

The University of Chicago

As at the University of Denver, organized programs in international relations began at the University of Chicago under the stimulus of a special foundation.[3] The Harris Foundation, designed to explore questions of international relations, was established at Chicago under the direction of a committee of the faculty in 1923. Annual conferences have been held since on topics of current international interest, each consisting of public lectures, often by distinguished visitors from public life in the United States and abroad, and round-table discussions by experts. Some forty published volumes as well as mimeographed reports have resulted from these conferences.

The committee's work early aroused student interest in world affairs at Chicago, and in response to student requests, the faculty committee, in 1926, published a special listing of all the courses in the university bearing on international relations. This singling out of international relations courses was so effective in influencing student enrollments that it led to the establishment by the Division of Social Sciences in 1931 of the Committee on International Relations to supervise graduate studies in international relations and to recommend candidates for the master's and doctor's degrees in this field. This cross-disciplinary committee with power to accept candidates for advanced degrees, to supervise their work, and to recommend them for degrees was one of a series of such interdepartmental committees established as a part of a general reorganization of the university during that period. While most of the committee members were faculty members in academic departments, the Hutchins policy also emphasized the privilege of employing faculty members directly under the committee's authority. The interdisciplinary and independent character of the committee and its power to recom-

[3] For the information here reported, the author is deeply indebted to Quincy Wright, Bert Hoselitz, and other members of the University of Chicago faculty.

mend candidates for degrees were academic developments closely related to a widespread effort in the United States to reduce departmental barriers and isolations.

The University of Chicago committee was an able group, led by Professor Quincy Wright, a noted scholar deeply devoted to the training of young scholars in international affairs. Under his direction and almost as a direct outgrowth of his ability and devotion, the committee guided the advanced studies of a notable group of young men during more than a quarter of a century. Among these are men now serving as distinguished academic figures and as leaders in public affairs, research, and government service.

Certain inadequacies in the structure of the Chicago program, however, began to appear, which led to changes in the late 1940's. Even with access to the Harris Foundation, the committee at no time had adequate funds with which to discharge its duties; the heavy tasks of advising students in the committee program had to be borne by men who were already overburdened with departmental responsibilities in their own disciplines. While there was a steadily increasing number of courses bearing on international relations offered in various departments of the university, no basic pattern in the program outlined for individual students emerged. The distinction between required and elective elements among course offerings covering an extensive and undefined field was blurred; in efforts to meet student interests, fringe courses on occasion became central courses. The interdependence of the programs for studying the basic disciplines of international relations—international law, international politics, international organization, diplomatic history, the psychology of international relations, and the programs for world area studies which developed rapidly in the United States during the 1940's—added to the complexities of the Chicago committee's operations.

By the end of World War II and in view of the rapid growth of international programs in a number of other universities, a careful re-examination of the pattern at Chicago was deemed desirable. In 1949, Edward Meade Earle, Princeton scholar in international studies and a leading member of the board of the Denver foundation, was asked by the faculty and administration at Chicago to make an appraisal of the university's program. At the same time, Professor Wright secured questionnaire evaluations of the program from its alumni. On the basis of these questionnaires and of a wide range of consultations, Professor Earle recommended (*a*) that the course offerings of the program be carefully reconsidered, with preference for a basic required set of courses and a reduction of fringe electives, (*b*) that committee responsibility for directing graduate work could be permanently successful only if a full-time director were provided for the committee's work, and (*c*) that the Ph.D. program be returned to the appropriate departments of the social sciences, leaving to the Committee on International Relations a program leading to the master's degree. The last recommendation was made in view of the reported difficulties of holders of the Ph.D. in international relations in securing positions, particularly in academic institutions which were ordinarily organized in departments corresponding to the traditional scholarly disciplines. Dr. Earle paid high tribute to the Chicago program and particularly to its leadership by Quincy Wright but felt that the program required more staff and funds than the university had been able to provide for it.

On the retirement of Professor Wright, the university adopted Professor Earle's recommendation that a full-time director of studies be appointed. Professor Bert Hoselitz held the post until 1958 and effected another of Professor Earle's recommendations—the development of a basic core curriculum, rooted in a concept of international relations as an academic field of study, leading to the master's degree. In 1956, steps were taken to follow the third of the Earle recommendations by gradually eliminating the separate doctorate in international relations, but this has remained a controversial matter. The Chicago pattern has become a high-level program of established courses, with reasonable provision for electives, leading to the degree of Master in International Relations. The core program embraces courses in international politics, international organization, international law, American and European diplomacy, and the economic aspects of international relations. Students seeking their master's degree are under the academic jurisdiction of the Committee on International Relations. Further work leading to the doctorate, though with an emphasis on international relations, is in the hands of the departments devoted to the various social science disciplines.

The program of the University of Denver, developing roughly during the same years as that at Chicago embraced an instructional offering at the undergraduate and graduate levels, but also reached out into the problems of handling foreign students, of supporting individual research, and of developing the role of the university in educating the public about international matters. The committee at Chicago was largely concerned with direct instruction, the initiation of large-scale research enterprises, and such research matters as were involved in the individual training of graduate students. For these purposes, the pattern of an interdepartmental committee was adequate, but it failed to embrace other international interests of the university. The growing number of foreign students who arrived at the University of Chicago were cared for by other agencies and offices of the university. Later a major International House was established on the campus as a relatively autonomous unit, perhaps not adequately related even to the existing student unions. A separate and highly important Center for Comparative Studies in Education was organized in the 1950's. A very considerable range of foundation and government-supported enterprises was undertaken by different and unrelated faculty groups, but the Committee on International Relations remained almost exclusively an agency concerned with instruction and a limited area of research.

Neither the Chicago committee nor the Denver foundation dealt directly with the university's own international relations or responsibilities of a cultural and scholarly character, or with the administration of major group research, or with the service tasks —both praiseworthy and problem-arousing—widely assumed by academic institutions under government contract or foundation support. In both institutions pioneering paths had been opened, but sources of personnel and finance were not sufficient to follow through permanently on a comprehensive basis.

There developed at Chicago even more than at Denver a multiplicity of programs needing, in some degree at least, policy analysis and administrative coordination. Inherent in these developments at Denver and Chicago were problems focused on the desirable degree of coordination among all campus activities related to international affairs and interests. Should undergraduate and graduate activities be in any degree interrelated? Should matters of instruction and research be involved in the machinery by which a dynamic extracurricular program for students is developed and maintained? Can an over-all policy for an institution be developed which leaves administrative implementation to autonomous units? Certain assumptions about such questions as these were doubtless in the minds of the pioneers at Denver and Chicago, but neither the validation of the assumptions nor the pressures giving prominence to the questions themselves were characteristic of the years between World Wars I and II.

Stanford University

Stanford University illustrates excellently the way in which international interests develop in a variety of academic locations.[4] The university was a pioneer in Asia studies, as befits its West Coast location; courses on Far Eastern history were offered at Stanford as early as 1936. Russian studies were developed early

[4] For much of the data here reported the author is indebted to conversations with various members of the Stanford faculty and administrative staff. In particular I am indebted to Paul Hanna, Ronald Hilton, Carl B. Spaeth, and Vice-Provost Robert J. Wert. A variety of papers and pamphlets, many of them dealing with the Hoover Institution on War, Revolution, and Peace, have been examined.

under the impetus of Harold Fisher's research interests. In similar fashion, Latin American studies made early headway under the influence of John C. Branner, Percy Martin, and Graham Stuart. The Food Research Institute at Stanford had unique international ramifications, and the Stanford Research Institute, established later as a semiautonomous unit located in Menlo Park, has dealt with the interrelations of economics and education on an international scale.

The developments at Stanford were dramatically influenced by the establishment there of the Hoover Institution on War, Revolution, and Peace. During World War I, while Hoover was serving as chairman of the Commission for Relief in Belgium, he became interested in the collection of records relating to the war. This interest grew and he turned to his friend, Ray Lyman Wilbur, president of Stanford, for counsel and assistance. As a result of their conversations, Dr. E. D. Adams, professor of history at Stanford, was placed in charge of a staff which was maintained in Europe by Mr. Hoover for the purpose of accumulating documents and records when he became Director General of Relief for the Allied and Associated Powers in 1918. It was a favorable climate and circumstance for collecting, and unusual and extensive collections were accumulated. In the early 1920's the housing of the collections became a problem, and again in consultation with President Wilbur, arrangements were made for depositing the materials at Stanford University.

Development of the Hoover Institution and its library was shaped by the personal friendship of Hoover and Wilbur. The institution was set up as a virtually autonomous unit to manage the library, to sponsor research, to facilitate the use of the library by research scholars from all over the world, and to develop such instructional programs as seemed desirable. By 1941 a special building—the impressive Hoover Tower—was constructed on the Stanford campus to house the institution and its library. But the exact interrelations between the institution, the library, the departments of the university, and other Stanford projects in international affairs was not made completely clear. These relations were not difficult so far as the use of the library was concerned, but as the established social science departments and the area-interested groups in the university intensified their own instruction in international affairs, problems became sharper and more difficult. In a sense, the initially unplanned relationship of the institution and the university became an obstacle to coordinated development of an international program at Stanford.

In the meantime a wide range of interests had appeared at Stanford, unrelated organically or in policy terms to the institution. Course offerings bearing on international matters were substantially increased, sometimes overlapping the instructional offerings beginning to take form at the institution. Stanford became a major center for the reception of foreign students and early established an office for the advisement of such students. The American students at Stanford developed as a phase of their extracurricular program, a student Institute of International Relations. The institute is

> a student organized and operated society which grew from a series of casual discussion groups into what is now (1962) the largest and most comprehensive international club in any American university. Aside from its regular programs, the IIR works constantly to create more effective relationships between American and Foreign students on the Stanford campus, and its Conference Division annually conducts a foreign-policy institute, recently expanded into a five-day conference with distinguished speakers, nightly seminars, and extensive background preparation. The Institute maintains its own library, and operates a Stanford Overseas Information Service which assists American students planning vacations, study, or careers abroad. The IIR also provides more than 200 California high schools with programs and materials on international problems and publishes a bimonthly newsletter.[5]

In the research fields bearing on defense and foreign operations, Stanford, particularly through its professional schools, undertook a wide variety of enterprises. The Graduate School

[5] Memorandum prepared by Carl B. Spaeth, dean, School of Law, Stanford University, 1962.

of Business developed a program for training management personnel which reached seventeen countries, and is now conducting summer programs in Iran, Ceylon, New Zealand, and Ethiopia. The School of Engineering conducts similarly far-reaching assignments with courses in Ceylon and Spain, and research enterprises in Australia, Switzerland, Argentina, and Holland. The School of Education, particularly through its then dean, Grayson Kefauver, was instrumental in helping to establish Unesco and has, since the war, developed a substantial program in comparative education. The Stanford Institute of Communications Research under Wilbur Schramm has been heavily involved in national programs of international cultural relations. By the late 1950's Stanford had embarked on a program by which off-campus centers were established in France, Germany, and Italy and study centers in Tokyo and Taiwan as aids in the international education of university students, both undergraduate and graduate.

These activities, as in most universities, developed out of individual, small group, and departmental interests. These were ordinarily unrelated or casually related to one another, and by the end of the decade of the 1950's Stanford felt seriously the need for a more systematic structural arrangement. A Committee on International Studies, created in 1953, had not functioned adequately, and the relations of the Hoover Institution to the rest of the university continued to be perplexing. In 1959, the university Board of Trustees passed a series of resolutions which recognized the Hoover Institution as an autonomous unit within the university under the leadership of a director holding administrative rather than academic tenure and responsible to the president; the institution's management of its library and of research based on the library was recognized, but its instructional responsibilities were minimized.

Of major importance, the Committee on International Studies was revitalized and its functions expanded. The committee, operating as an adjunct of the president's office, was charged with handling questions arising from programs or program-proposals related to international relations and involving instruction, research, contracts and services, foundation grants, and student affairs. It is essentially a committee on policy and coordination. For a time the provost served as its chairman. He was succeeded by Professor Emile Desfres, and in 1962 Professor Carl Spaeth, former dean of the School of Law, was made chairman. With half his time devoted to the committee's work, Dean Spaeth is moving rapidly toward a significantly new level of policy formulation and reasonable coordination of the university's wide range of international concerns.

Columbia University

Columbia University's interest in international matters is long standing, and was particularly cultivated during the administration of President Nicholas Murray Butler, vigorous champion of "the international mind," first president of the Carnegie Endowment for International Peace, and himself a force in the public affairs of America and Europe. Located at a twentieth-century crossroads of international contacts, Columbia early felt the winds which dispersed American isolationism. It became a center for the study of international law; pioneering studies in comparative education were developed at Columbia Teachers College in the years immediately following World War I. The university was one of the first to move toward regional studies in world affairs. By World War II, Columbia was host to greater numbers of foreign students and scholars than any other American university.

The major and systematic development of Columbia's organized program in international studies,[6] however, came just after World War II and had its direct genesis in the Naval

[6] L. Gray Cowan, *A History of the School of International Affairs and Associated Area Institutes*, prepared for the bicentennial history of Columbia University (New York: Columbia University Press, 1954), 106 pp. For this account, the author is also indebted to conversations with Schuyler Wallace, Gray Cowan, and other members of the Columbia staff.

School of Military Government and Administration which operated at Columbia during the war. Its rise was markedly influenced by the needs of government and industry for personnel trained in contemporary issues of international relations, by the rapid rise of world area studies, and by the academic problems of coordination among disciplines concerned with world relations. In 1944–45, proposals took concrete form at Columbia for the creation of a graduate professional school which would train personnel for international work and would serve as a facilitating and coordinating agency for the international interests of academic departments and certain envisaged area institutes.

The new School of International Affairs was formally established in 1945 under the directorship of Professor Schuyler Wallace [7] and with the strong support of the president of the university. As at Denver and at Chicago, the Columbia program is in many respects "the lengthened shadow of a man," in this case, Schuyler Wallace. Under his creative direction, the school was designed, not primarily for academic research, but for the professional training of operative personnel; it emphasized "the separation of the managerial or administrative side" of international relations "from its purely scholarly aspects" without any sacrifice of standards in training and achievement. The program of the school was made up largely of courses drawn from the discipline-based departments of the university. Programs for individual students developed from the school's functional approach to area institutes, and led to a master's degree. Language facility was emphasized. Approximately two years of language study were required for the master's degree—somewhat longer if the student secured both the degree and the certificate of one of the area institutes. No doctorate was offered by the school; the doctorate was reserved for academic departments but could be secured with specialization on international rela-

[7] Professor Wallace, relinquishing his directorship in 1962, was succeeded by Andrew W. Cordier, drawn from the United Nations Secretariat.

tions through the discipline involved. The school as a training center has been highly successful; its graduates are in government service and in business, both within the United States and abroad. In recent years an increasing number of foreign students have been admitted to the program, particularly selected groups of promising young foreign service officers drawn from the emerging nations.

The same faculty group which planned the School of International Affairs also planned a number of related area institutes. Each of these institutes focuses on a given area of the world; in each institute is assembled a group of scholars in "branches of human knowledge concerned with man as a social being, i.e., anthropology, business, economics, education, government, history, law, literature, psychology, religion, and sociology." Most of these scholars were drawn from departments of the university, and all new members of institute staffs were also appointed within departments. It is important that even if a faculty appointment to a department for service in an institute was made possible by temporary financial aid from a foundation, the university guaranteed tenure for such scholars, pledging general university funds in this commitment. This provision made possible a permanence and a caliber of personnel for the institutes which might have been impossible had their entire support rested on special nonpermanent foundation grants.

In 1946, the Russian Institute was established at Columbia under a grant from the Rockefeller Foundation. In 1948, the East Asian Institute was established with financial help from the same source. The European Institute came into operation in 1949, under aid from the Carnegie Corporation. In 1952, the Near and Middle East Institute was created, and this was followed in 1962 by a Latin American Institute. Two additional "programs" have been developed—one on African studies and one on East Central Europe studies—which may, with adequate financing, become institutes. While each of these institutes and programs has developed "its own purpose and style," they are all intimately interrelated through the School of International Affairs. Their programs and budgets and appointments are reviewed by the director of the school. Moreover, these programs work closely with long-established graduate departments in the faculties of political science and philosophy. Indeed, the close meshing of academic department and regional or international specialization is a distinguishing feature of Columbia's area programs: members of the institute staffs and officers of instruction in the School of International Affairs are also members of graduate departments giving instruction in the social sciences and humanities. Regional training is not in conflict with, or an alternative to, command of an academic discipline. All students in the institutes, before being accepted as candidates for an institute certificate, must be candidates for an advanced degree in an appropriate department of the graduate faculties or in the School of International Affairs.

Although a first function of the regional institutes as well as of the school is that of training personnel for management and administration of international activities, it is also true that the program has produced many academic leaders. A second function is that of research, particularly in the institutes. There is a steady flow of research publications from individual faculty members, and in addition various large-scale group research projects have been developed under the sponsorship and direction of one of the institutes or of the school. Studies on *Men and Politics in Continental China, Economics Behind the Iron Curtain, A Chinese Oral History Project,* and *Studies on Hungary* illustrate those completed or under way. These have been financed under special research grants, negotiated and administered through the director of the school and his advisory board.

In general, then, the structure which has taken form at Columbia since 1945 has the School of International Studies at its center, with the school's director and administrative board as coordinating agents for the interrelations with area institutes and graduate academic departments. Certain units other than area institutes are closely related to the school as, for example, the Council on Atomic Age Studies, established in 1957. An Institute of War and Peace Studies exists as a purely research unit. The scope of responsibility of the school extends over instruction and research, and, in connection with some projects, reception and advisement of particular students. The school has had only limited responsibility in the field of governmental contracts; other units of the university have developed their own programs. Columbia Teachers College, for example, has its own coordinator of grants and projects in international activity. The School of International Affairs has no responsibility for most of the hundreds of foreign students who attend Columbia each year or for such extracurricular influences as International House or the lectures and programs arranged for undergraduates. It has had little planned influence on the undergraduate college or, until recently, on the professional schools of Columbia.

Within its sphere of responsibility, however, the school and its institutes serve an essential function of planning and coordination. Institutes do not "just grow" at Columbia; there is, indeed, a large measure of planning in the addition of internationally minded personnel throughout the university. A continuous review of functions and needs is maintained. This basically important function of coordinated planning and review has recently been further safeguarded at Columbia by the creation of a university-wide Committee on International Studies. The administrative board of the School of International Affairs has been replaced by a faculty in international studies, composed of all faculty members attached to the school. The new, university-wide committee is chaired by the president of the university; its vice-chairman is the director of the School of International Affairs. Attached to it is an executive secretary who has been recently designated as "coordinator of international studies," with special responsibilities for planning and raising funds for a building to house "such university activities in the international field as would benefit by being located in one building." The scope of the committee's operations is likely to be determined within the framework of planning the envisaged physical center for international activities, but its establishment represents a significant movement among universities for more systematic planning and policy-determination in this area. It is, in some ways, comparable to the central policy committee established at Stanford about the same time.

One influence leading to the establishment of an over-all committee at Columbia in 1960 was a change in policy of the Ford Foundation concerning certain grants in the international field —a constructive, farsighted policy which also markedly influenced developments at Harvard, California, Stanford, and a widening number of other universities. The foundation determined in 1960 to make grants, usually quite substantial in amount, to universities for the support of international relations programs, but expected the determination of priorities for the internal distribution of the grants to be effected by the institutions themselves. This policy threw back upon the universities the necessity of thinking through university-wide operations in this field, and increased the necessity for formulation of university policy and priority in program operations. The foundation policy seems to have contributed, at least indirectly, to the internal analysis and planning for developments in this field, which are, and should be, the proper responsibility of a university in a free society. It has emphasized the importance of over-all policy determination by the universities themselves.

Harvard University

The years since World War II have provided striking developments on university campuses all over the United States, of which Harvard, among the other institutions taking pre-eminence in this field, is a noteworthy example. The compactness, wealth, faculty personnel, and distinctive academic and corporate framework of Harvard make it somewhat less representative as an example of general developments in higher education than most other American institutions, but its approach to the development of and gradual coordination of international interests is interesting and significant. In essence, the Harvard record emphasizes reliance on the individual initiative of able faculty members and stress upon research and the facilitation of research; even in these areas, however, its organizational pattern, in over-all terms, is more fluid and less structured than in institutions which are larger and administratively more complex.

Shortly after World War II, Harvard developed an M.A. program in international relations, interdepartmental in character. This program shortly declined, and primary attention shifted to the work of a group of professors—Kluckhohn in anthropology, Allport in psychology, for example—whose wartime experiences in cultural analysis and propaganda influences had broken new intellectual ground. These interests led to establishment of a Department of Social Relations, concerned, among other interests, with the relations of people of differing cultures across national boundary lines. Kluckhohn's studies, animated in part by the national frustrations in negotiating with the Soviet Union, led to establishment of a Soviet Union Program developed under a Committee on Regional Studies, which was analogous to the development of the area programs at Columbia. Paralleling this was a Russian Research Center, focusing on doctoral and postdoctoral studies and emphasizing interdisciplinary contacts. These contacts, effected not only by regular seminars of scholars, but also by proximity of offices, a common library, and the informality of group meals, proved extremely rewarding. Since these two developments overlapped, their administration was gradually combined, and the entire program evolved so far as academic policy was concerned, under the Committee on Regional Studies.

The nature and extent of growth along these lines at Harvard are emphasized in the report of President Pusey for the academic year 1960–1961. In that report he says:

For several decades—perhaps longer—there has slowly been growing in Harvard a sense that her mission is world-wide. This is not to question Harvard's essential rootage in this nation, it is rather simply to recognize that the present activities, interests, and responsibilities of our country, and so also of her educational institutions reach round the world. . . . The development of area studies, in which scholars from various disciplines join efforts, in training and in research, to achieve a broad and deep understanding of a particular cultural area, has been a conspicuous feature of academic activity in the United States since World War II. Our first venture of this kind was the establishment early in 1948 of the Russian Research Center. In 1954, there was added a Center for Middle Eastern Studies; and more recently, in 1957, a Center for East Asian Studies. Each of these has its own "faculty" and its own program of both training and research. There is also here, a Center for International Affairs designed primarily to meet the needs, for further study, of individuals who in our Department of State and in various foreign offices already carry important responsibility for the maintenance of peace and order, and for development in the world. The research activity of this Center is directed toward basic problems of world politics.

In addition to all these, there came into existence last year a new kind of Center for Latin American Studies. This is not a highly organized unit as the others are, but, so far, simply an informal association of scholars from various faculties of the University who have come together largely on their own initiative to quicken University-wide interest in Latin America, to explore ways in which knowledge of the area can be increased here, and to seek opportunities by which the University may relate itself more constructively to this very important part of our hemisphere.

A center of still a different kind is the Center for International Legal Studies at the Law School. . . . This development in one department of one faculty of the University, which could in some degree be duplicated in many others, will serve to suggest the kinds of changes and the broadened outlook now being elicited in virtually every section of Harvard's activity because of widening intellectual interest and the growing irreversible interfusion of American and world affairs.

There are other random items from the accounts of the past year which accentuate this impression of broadened concern at Harvard. A new home for the Center for the Study of World Religions was formally opened at the Divinity School. The School of Public Health, which has long devoted a larger percentage of its effort to world problems perhaps than any other department of the University, acquired and brought into operation its Henry Lee Shattuck International House.[8]

In addition to these variously organized centers and activities, President Pusey comments on the 2,052 foreign students and scholars who were resident at Harvard in 1960–61; on the scholarship programs set up for them; on the scholars from other countries who are now permanently on the Harvard faculty; on the services of Harvard's sons in countries around the world; and on the widening of subject-matter interests and courses under the impact of America's widened horizons; on the Harvard Glee Club's 1960–61 tour through Asia; on student volunteer services in Tanganyika; and on Harvard's participation in the training of Peace Corps volunteers. A separate report deals with *Harvard and the Federal Government*[9]—a penetrating, over-all analysis of federal financial assistance to programs of research and training developed basically in the interests of national defense under contemporary conditions. These various, far-flung academic and service developments at Harvard are coordinated more by the compactness of the university governance, by the informality of continuing conversations among specialist scholars, and by the overview of the president's office than by the more carefully structured designs which seem desirable in most other major American universities.

Informal consultation among interested, individual scholars, operating within the context set by the Harvard Corporation and by the compactness and smallness of Cambridge, then, evolved academic policy and effected a degree of coordination among a variety of committees and centers. The work of these individuals and groups was primarily at the graduate level, and with re-

[8] Nathan Pusey, *The President's Report: Harvard University: 1960–1961* (Cambridge, Mass.: Harvard University, 1962), pp. 5–8.

[9] Cambridge, Mass.: Harvard University, 1961.

sources which made possible unusual focus on research. The results are impressive in terms of scholarship, but do not set examples in the formal determination of over-all institutional policy or in systematic and long-range planning.

Michigan State University

A different approach to the establishment and administration of university programs in international affairs developed during the 1950's at Michigan State University, built upon the concept of a land-grant institution with a long and highly successful experience with extension programs of public service. In these programs Michigan State has been deeply involved in the developmental concerns of its state, particularly in agriculture and the application of knowledge to social and community development. Its skill in off-campus, developmental operations was an obvious asset as the Federal Government became involved in aid to underdeveloped areas of the world, and Michigan State University was early called upon to carry out developmental enterprises abroad, in its areas of particular competence, under governmental contract.

Academic study of international affairs was already established at Michigan State. The doctorate was offered in international relations; a number of programs for training foreign service personnel had been developed; research abroad in their areas of specialization was frequently undertaken by faculty members. Within the unique tradition of the land-grant university, these academic interests were early combined with the opportunities inherent in overseas operations undertaken as implementation of governmental foreign policy. Academic interests and field-service activities vitalized one another under the genius of the institution's president, John A. Hannah, and the energy of an unusual assemblage of young and creative faculty. Unlike the developments at Chicago and Columbia, for example, the program included from the outset unquestioned commitment to overseas operation on the part of Michigan State, and also included full utilization of such overseas operation for the academic concerns in the international dimensions of higher education.

Faced with administrative tasks and policy decisions requiring immediate action, the president of the university in 1955 established the post of dean of international programs and called Glen L. Taggart from the sociology department to the position. His functions were not only to supervise the international operations in which the university was or might be involved but also to exercise leadership in relating these operations to the academic interests of the institution, to stimulate further growth in the academic studies related to international affairs, and to aid in discerning more clearly the university's proper role in the international field.

Of particular importance has been the development at Michigan State of a university-wide study of the institution's posture and function in international matters, perhaps the most comprehensive study of such character thus far made by any university in the world. Shortly after his appointment, the dean of international programs organized a faculty Committee on the Role of the University in International Programs. It was designed to make an institutional analysis in the same pattern as those undertaken in the program of the Carnegie Endowment for International Peace. Out of discussions in this committee emerged a plan for involving large numbers of the faculty, in all departments, in an analysis of "the international dimension of Michigan State University." The Ford Foundation granted financial aid for the study. A faculty-administration steering committee was brought together to identify the high priority areas of international character with which the university should be concerned. Then study seminars, each composed of faculty members released from some of their regular work to participate in the seminars, met regularly during the spring and summer of 1958. In the autumn of that year their various reports were completed and reviewed by the steering committee. An Integrating Seminar Committee worked over the seminar reports. And in 1959 a policy statement for the whole institution was issued, embodying recommendations concerning developments which have since become the basis for university action.[10] Chapters of the report deal with (1) International Challenges to University Education, (2) Areas of Special Concern to Higher Education in the United States, (3) Recommendations Directly Affecting Teaching Programs, (4) Recommended Research Expansion, (5) Influencing the General Culture through University Extension, and (6) Structuring the University.

Within the framework of this policy report, Michigan State University has moved from preoccupation with foreign projects to on-campus emphases in instruction, academic development, research, faculty involvement in foreign affairs almost as a planned program of in-service faculty education, and the cultivation of an international climate on the campus as a whole. Many of the results are impressive, though others may be criticized. But, for the purposes of discussion here, the significant fact is that a new administrative approach and structure, originating in field service operations in underdeveloped foreign areas, led to comprehensive institutional self-scrutiny, specific formulation of policy, and development of desired academic strengths. The administrative structure which emerges from this situation is distinctly worth examination.

The Michigan State report begins its discussion of university organization by observing that

> In structuring an international dimension to the University which takes account of the interrelations between the American society and the rest of the world, it is necessary to have imaginative and flexible arrangements. Structures need to be geared to a midway course between overspecialization and over-dispersion. On the one hand, international affairs must not become the sole responsibility of a number

[10] Michigan State University, *Towards an International Dimension at Michigan State University* (Mimeographed report; August 1959).

of specialists isolated from the rest of the university. Such a procedure limits from the start the opportunities of influencing large groups of students and adult citizens. Nor should the work become diffused thinly throughout the institution with no particular center of responsibility or abiding interest. This procedure leads to the twin dangers of superficiality and low priority. Thus, while the University should strive for widespread involvement, it also needs to develop special cores of interest intimately related to the international problems, and with a responsible administrative officer interested both in breadth of programs and in depth of analysis. . . .

. . . .

To avoid the twin dangers of excess isolation and over-diffusiveness, specific responsibilities for considering particular phases of the international role must be allocated in various locations throughout the University with coordination and stimulation in some central office. There must be a clearly defined role and special responsibility residing in this office, but it should not be conceived as having sole responsibility for all programs dealing with the interrelations between cultures. Still, the diffused local areas of responsibility must be brought together, to interact with each other in such a way as to encourage the growth of competent scholars with the ability to perform as generalists.[11]

The report concerns itself with alterations in tenure regulations, retirement and sabbatical provisions, and promotion procedures as they affect foreign service for faculty members, a matter still inadequately dealt with in most universities. Although originating in the institution's concern with foreign service programs, the report is also concerned with the development of academic structures and specializations and research facilities which are or may be related to such foreign service. It is genuinely concerned with the international dimension of the university in its total impact on students. With these factors in mind, the report recommended establishment at Michigan State of a center for international studies.[12]

However, the stimulating and coordinating purpose envisaged for the center has actually been achieved through less formal administrative arrangements, and the center has not been created.

[11] *Ibid.*, pp. 134–36.
[12] *Ibid.*, p. 145.

A campuswide committee, including representatives from the various colleges and other academic units of the university, has been established as advisory to the dean of international programs. This committee serves as an effective policy-making and coordinating agency. Under its stimulus, the university has recently entered on a program of area studies, with centers on Africa, Asia, and Latin America already created. A parallel series of functional centers, exploring the adjustments of academic specialties to developmental needs, have also been created. A major revision of the undergraduate offerings in social science has been effected, with substantially increased additions of international matters to the liberal arts program. Graduate-student research studies have been unusually effectively related to overseas operations, and the overseas operations have themselves been shaped to contribute to academic concern.

The office of the dean of international programs is at once the spearhead for university adjustments under the impact of international affairs, and also the facilitator of academic concerns with instruction and research which in most universities take precedence over service functions. The Michigan State development is a significant pioneering enterprise, demonstrative of the realism and vitality inherent in the concept of the land-grant university. The record from Lansing is one of the distinctive chapters in the story of adjustment in American higher education to international affairs.

University of California, Los Angeles

Many of the factors and forces referred to in these case examples of institutional administrative evolutions have influenced the recent establishment of an Institute for International and Foreign Studies at the University of California, Los Angeles. The institute, created in 1958, emerged from the university's interests in area studies. For many years, a cross-departmental Committee on Latin American Studies had existed on the Los

Angeles campus. The committee brought together specialists in the social sciences and humanities who were concerned with Latin America. It stimulated growth in the area study, carried on or facilitated research enterprises, and issued reports and publications. After World War II, a comparable Committee on African Studies emerged on the campus. With rising general interest in African matters, the committee operated not only as a coordinating and stimulating agency, but actively supported research and faculty travel and scholarship awards under the impetus of foundation grants which it was instrumental in securing. It took the initiative for the university in expanding African studies and in negotiating with governmental and foundation agencies for projects and services abroad. A further Committee on Middle East Studies developed in the university. The need for a degree of coordination among these area committees, comparable to that provided at Columbia by the School of International Affairs, led at UCLA to the establishment of an Institute for International and Foreign Studies.

The report of a faculty committee [13] which recommended establishment of the institute outlined nine functions it should serve: (1) promotion of research; (2) coordination, encouragement, and development of interdepartmental studies and centers; (3) maintenance of an information center on international matters for university use; (4) liaison with diplomatic and consular officials; (5) planning of university hospitality for foreign visitors; (6) promotion of public programs on international matters for the university community; (7) facilitation of international exchanges of students and faculty; (8) liaison with international relations activities of the Los Angeles area; and (9) advice and assistance on recruitment of university personnel for international service. The director of the institute, Robert G. Neumann, professor of political science, is its chief administra-

[13] Robert G. Neumann (chairman), mimeographed statement on the *Creation of an Institute for International and Foreign Studies,* June 7, 1956.

tive officer. He is aided by an Advisory Committee, whose members are drawn from academic departments and professional schools and include the chairmen of all interdepartmental area centers. The committee is set up to serve as a coordinating council for all the campus international concerns under the wide-ranging functions of the institute.

In one sense, the institute is a holding company for the area studies groups; these groups, earlier organized as committees, are now set up as more formal centers, each composed of members drawn from a wide range of academic departments. But the institute has wider functions. One of its first enterprises was the preparation of a roster of university personnel indicating competencies such as language facility or familiarity with various areas of the world. This manpower roster has been useful, not only in university planning but also as a catalogue of resource specialists for government and foundation agencies. The institute has convened special colloquia, ordinarily on an invitational basis, for the analysis of issues of foreign policy or international relations. It has encouraged the development of comparative studies, as in education or public administration or law. It has counseled in the development of a program in comparative education, including the negotiation of two AID contracts for service in Nigeria under that program. It directs a program, financed by the government, for serving Fulbright grantees in southern California. It arranges for the reception of foreign visitors and distributes a roster of foreign visitors to the university. It serves as a clearinghouse of information concerning foreign study or employment.

Typical of the institute's service function—the planning, stimulating, and coordinating of legitimate university enterprises—is its work in connection with research. In the report of the faculty committee which led to creation of the institute, it was suggested:

> The Institute for International and Foreign Studies should encourage and promote studies in cooperation with the University Research

> Committee, the University Library Committee, and the Graduate Council. It should review projects submitted to it for advisability, practicability, and feasibility. It should then aid these projects, where appropriate, by assisting in contacting foundations, research institutions, or government agencies which are in a position to grant financial aid. A constant liaison with such foundations and agencies would constitute an important function of the Institute.[14]

In carrying out this function, the institute made the beginnings of development of research policy; it aids in screening the research proposals which are put forward in the name of the university and in effecting adequate coordination of research enterprises.

Unlike the Committee on International Relations at Chicago or the School of International Affairs at Columbia, the institute at UCLA does not itself offer degrees. The area centers maintain, through academic departments, programs of instruction which provide opportunity for advanced degrees through departmental channels and are now offering in some cases area-based degrees at the master's level. The main potentials of the institute lie in its alertness to matters affecting the university's program in international affairs, its continuing review of policies and proposals, and its operation as a facilitating service for a widely scattered group of undertakings. Its weaknesses lie in a number of matters. It is attached to the undergraduate college rather than directly to the chancellor's office for administrative and budget purposes. The institute has little to do with foreign students, although there are large numbers of such students at UCLA, and rather extensive administrative arrangements have to be made for their selection, reception, and counseling. The institute has only the loosest responsibility for development of academic programs, including area studies, the promotion of language studies, and direct instruction in international relations. It has less power for coordination than have the recently established committees at Stanford and Columbia, nor has it the allocation of faculty and

[14] *Ibid.*, p. 3.

secretarial time that those committees have. The institute is a major step in the right direction, but in some respects not adequate for the university interests it serves.

Other Institutional Experiences

A number of institutions have established in recent years offices for handling international services arising from sources other than graduate academic departments. The University of Texas, for example, has long had scholarly concerns with international matters, particularly in connection with Latin American studies. An office of foreign student adviser was set up after World War II and, in 1951, this office was expanded into an "International Office" handling a wider range of matters. It handles the reception and advisement of foreign students, Fulbright and related activities for Texas students and faculty who study or teach abroad, and foreign contracts with a number of countries arranged through AID or other governmental agencies. The Director of the International Office has responsibility for directing some activities, supervising others, and coordinating all enterprises involving interchange of personnel. Within its sphere the office increases administrative efficiency, though it has not moved toward integration of the university's external relations with its programs of instruction and research to the degree that has been sought at Michigan State University.

The concept of an international office such as that at Texas has been adopted in various other universities. By 1961, at least twenty institutions had established such offices under varying names, and a considerably larger number of institutions were actively exploring the possibilities of closer relationship between the handling of foreign students and the other international enterprises of the campus. At Syracuse University, the Maxwell Graduate School of Citizenship and Public Affairs developed special programs for training foreign-service personnel and became the coordinating center for much of the university's rapidly expanding concerns in the international area. Georgetown University has long maintained a program concerned with preparing personnel for foreign service, and its language program, including study of English as a second tongue, has been outstanding.

In the spring of 1962, the University of Pittsburgh began a comprehensive analysis of its program in relation to world affairs. The Graduate School of Public and International Affairs, under the direction of Donald C. Stone, offers at Pittsburgh a program for administrators which draws heavily on a variety of disciplines. An Office of Cultural and Educational Affairs deals with a wide range of extracurricular matters related to international understanding. The director of this office, Shepherd Whitman, now serves as chairman of an all-university committee which is directing an institutional study, carried out by faculty task forces in every department and school of the university. The study covers matters of teaching and research, the time schedule for further development, and the analysis of goals and resources. As announced by Chancellor Edward Litchfield at the 1962 commencement ceremonies:

We are prepared to postulate an international dimension as a constant in our academic planning, our budgeting, our building and our staffing . . . we will anticipate:

1. Systematic review of our individual and interdisciplinary curricula with careful attention to the incorporation of all pertinent cross and comparative cultural materials.
2. A planned increase in the number of our faculty who come to us from abroad.
3. The creation of maximum opportunities for our faculty to enjoy ever broader international experience.
4. An acceleration and broadening of educational programs and scholarly pursuits abroad when we can be of useful service to our own and foreign governments.
5. A determined effort to reinvest the knowledge gained from service abroad in the ongoing program of the university . . .
6. An appreciable extension of our present general and professional training for Americans who will be engaged in governmental, business, and educational activities abroad.

7. A far greater attention to the needs of the undergraduate, graduate, and professional student who may come to us from abroad.[15]

One of the most promising phases of the Pittsburgh program is the development of a Regional Council for International Education. Composed of thirty-one colleges and universities within a radius of two hundred fifty miles of Pittsburgh, the council provides for institutional cooperation in a wide range of efforts. It holds round-table discussions on comparative education for visiting foreign scholars, facilitates interchange of visiting academic personnel, develops special programs utilizing cooperatively the distinctive resources of each institution for the educational improvement of all. Its program, as now being developed, includes (1) establishment of a regional center for orientation of incoming foreign students, (2) coordinated development of such curriculum changes as areas studies, (3) interchange of foreign visitors, (4) cooperation in development of foreign programs "including student year, semester, or summers abroad, faculty seminars abroad, and assistance to AID, Peace Corps, and other national agencies," and (5) establishment of a clearinghouse center at Pittsburgh for the interchange of information about world affairs in education among the cooperating campuses.

With a commitment of this scope, the task force and central committee at Pittsburgh may be expected to open up new paths in university structure and organization.

The Necessity for Over-all University Policy

It is obvious from consideration of the administrative developments related to international concerns in these representative universities that no one pattern or structure can be universally recommended. But it is equally obvious that no university can afford to ignore the search for an administrative structure appropriate to its own traditions and interests and to the responsibilities it is called upon to discharge. In that search certain general

[15] Edward H. Litchfield, "Opening Remarks," University of Pittsburgh commencement, June 11, 1962, MS, pp. 2–3.

observations derived from the experience of American universities during the last forty years may be useful.

The first observation is that no sound and enduring administrative structure for handling international concerns can be developed except as the university itself—its faculty and its central administration—has analyzed the role it seeks to play in international matters. If the university restricts itself to research and instruction on matters international, it will develop one kind of organization. If it educates public servants in this field at professional levels, it must provide the machinery for a systematic relationship with government. And if it goes into service abroad in the interest of applied research, survey, foreign policy, or international development, it must create still more complex machinery. If the university drifts from one function or one enterprise to another, without a clear-cut policy to guide its action, then administrative confusion and waste of resources are almost certain to result. That has been, unfortunately, the situation on most campuses until very recently, and is the situation on many campuses now.

From this point of view, the systematic policy formulation undertaken at Michigan State University during an early stage in the development of its international programs is impressive. The various self-study programs on universities and international affairs carried out by some seventy colleges and universities under the encouragement of the Carnegie Endowment during the 1950's were steps in the right direction. It is eminently desirable for any university to appraise its resources, inventory its activities, and rationalize its policies and purposes in respect to international influences as a basis for discerning the guidelines and policy criteria most suited to its resources and its limitations. This preliminary analysis is an essential guide, but it should not, of course, become a rigid outlook. Continuing analysis and reexamination of policy is itself one of the essential elements of a wise policy.

In the analysis preliminary to policy formulation, the identification of all the elements in the university which should be involved is necessary. In virtually no institution to date have the bases of policy-making in this area been sufficiently broad. A policy-making committee should contain members competent to deal with questions concerning (1) the impact of international relations on the liberal arts program at the undergraduate level, (2) the graduate program for prospective specialists in international relations, including the organized area studies, (3) research on international matters, (4) the selection and treatment of foreign students, (5) faculty interchange, (6) participation in the university's own network of foreign relations in the academic and professional fields, (7) university enterprises abroad, (8) the management of governmental contracts and foundation grants in this area, and (9) the central administration of the university. A committee on policy which ignores any of these areas of interest is not likely to do full justice to the university's potential or to envisage an adequate administrative arrangement.

Committees representative of academic departments cannot adequately represent the professional schools; committees which do not include those responsible for foreign students or for the negotiation of governmental contracts are not adequate in developing an administrative operation touching these matters. While no perfect administrative structure is likely to emerge full-blown from the deliberations of a committee, progress toward that goal will be likelier if the committee is representative of all the interests which enter into the university policy. There has been growth toward this comprehensive committee within the institutions described in these pages. Starting with an operational program born of its agricultural extension program, Michigan State University has moved toward inclusion of academic specializations; starting with an academic committee embracing its institutes and area centers, Columbia has moved to include its professional schools and the administrative offices involved in contract negotiations.

The point of view to which this report is committed is that every major American university now has responsibilities of such scope and significance and complexity that comprehensive policy planning is essential. An inventory of the university's total activities and resources in the international field is the first step toward sound determination of policy. Instruction on international matters, world area studies, research, personnel training, faculty interchanges of an international nature, the handling of foreign students, field operations on "campuses abroad" or as related to foundation programs or to governmental enterprises, and the planned foreign study of American students are intimately interrelated and have joint as well as individual impact on the institution. Long-range planning by the university requires cooperative policy formulation among all these matters of interest. Unless there is a reasonable degree of coordination among them, the institution can easily become inconsistent within itself, fail to utilize its full resources, dissipate its efforts, or be wastefully involved in interoffice confusions or in continuing readjustments of program and of organization.

University Administration of International Activities

From the determination of university-wide purposes and policies by an adequately comprehensive committee should emerge plans for a continuing administrative arrangement. Experience suggests the advisability of not only an *ad hoc* appraising and policy-making committee, but also a continuing coordinating committee. This is what has evolved at Stanford, Columbia, the University of California, Los Angeles, and various other institutions. Such a standing committee attached directly to the central administration of the campus should represent faculty interests and should be small enough for continuing conversation among its members. It should operate within the framework of an established charter or directive such as may have been formulated by the *ad hoc* committee. It should maintain a continuing review of policy, should examine the interrelationships among relevant campus activities, should be alert to new possibilities and review new proposals, and should be the university's agency of external relations so far as international interests are concerned.

Such a committee cannot operate successfully without a director or executive officer of senior rank who gives virtually full time to its work. This has been demonstrated in all the university case studies that have been reviewed. The office will require a secretariat; it will often be expeditious to provide a central secretariat for this office which also serves various campus units concerned with international matters—the area centers, relevant research projects, management of interchange of persons, for example. Indeed, a central secretariat may not only be more economical and feasible, but also serve as a coordinating influence among relatively autonomous campus enterprises. If these services and agencies can be housed together, as is now planned for Columbia, the promise of effective coordination is all the greater.

The role of the director is a difficult one; he must stimulate activities without dominating them, must give negative advice on some proposals without being overcautious or bureaucratic, must maintain status within the society of scholars and at the same time devote much time to administration, must serve as chief liaison between the institution and the government, must keep channels of communication with foundations clear and uncluttered. He must have immediate access to the central administration of the campus and at the same time maintain close contacts with the university faculty.

Certain observations may be made concerning the financing of the administrative agency created around the director, whether it be an institute, a committee, an office, or a council. While most such agencies require outside financial aid, at least in their formative period, and the foundations have been generous in that aid for a number of institutions, it seems advantageous for the unit to be financed from the start, at least in part, from the regular budget of the university. The rapid growth of the institutes and area centers at Columbia was made possible, not only by substantial grants from the major foundations, but also by the willingness and ability of the university to commit its own funds by giving tenure appointments to scholars brought in on short-time grants. A number of promising developments in various colleges and universities have fallen by the wayside ultimately because there was no long-range effort at integrating budgets derived from special and terminal gifts with the ordinary financial resources and budgetary operations of the institution. The whole relationship of a university to world affairs, is, by the 1960's, sufficiently clear and convincing to warrant financial commitments from the university as well as from outside sources in any well-planned administrative arrangement for dealing with this field.

And, in a deeper than financial sense, the international affairs agency of the institution must be built soundly into the institution's permanent operation. Though it must have dynamic leadership, it cannot be dominating and cannot be built on temporary interests or the casual concerns of administration or staff. Long-term devotion and experience is essential for effective coordination of international academic matters. The prestige of academic rank gives greater effectiveness to the directing office and to the coordinating committee which is composed of faculty members from established disciplines rather than one composed of persons, no matter how able, not academically established within these disciplines. At the same time, academic personnel must be relieved of other activities if they are to function effectively as committee members, directors, researchers, or coordinators of projects. The recommended administrative arrangement requires a solid university commitment in terms of faculty time, budget, administrative support, and secretarial services. Under the policy coordination of such a committee and with the facilitation provided by its secretariat a wide range of operations may be conducted, each of which has a large degree of administrative autonomy. The adviser of foreign students, the office responsible for Fulbright applications, the faculty groups concerned with area studies, the departments or schools operating foreign contracts, the individuals and bureaus concerned with research bearing on international matters—all have their distinctive tasks, which may best be executed if they are interrelated within a policy framework and through the continuing conversations of a coordinating group.

Elements of a Campus Program

The first and major task of a coordinating committee, institute, or office is that of continuing analysis of the university activities which operate under the impact of world affairs. It should be a reviewing agency for new proposals, a stimulus to developments —both in research and instruction—which seem appropriate, a friendly watchdog on the activities already under way. Composed of responsible scholars and administrative officers, it should analyze university enterprises in terms of the discerned trends of academic life, the insights provided by research findings, the resources which exist within the institution or which may be made available, and the needs of the society in respect to foreign policy and international relations. In encouraging well-considered new developments and in discouraging ill-considered and hasty projects and reforms, the committee should play a major part in clarifying the role of the university in world affairs in a society which is by no means standing still.

This reviewing and stimulating task of the committee can be discharged wisely only if the committee is fully aware of the resources which exist within its university. For this reason the committee should maintain a roster of faculty personnel indicating the abilities and interests bearing on international matters of faculty members in all departments. What language facilities exist within the faculty? With what sections of the world are faculty members particularly well acquainted? What governmental or foreign experience resides within the total group? What personnel may be available for foreign assignment? Too frequently —particularly in the larger and more loosely organized institutions—the answers to such questions as these are left to chance. Yet, it is in terms of such resources that many policy decisions should be made. A roster of available talent such as that developed at UCLA may enable the institution to move more rapidly in meeting opportunities for development or may reveal resources on which new developments may be built. It may also lead to deeper consideration of the relation of foreign study, research, or assignment to such matters as tenure, promotion, retirement provisions, and sabbatical leaves. And such a roster is of obvious value to government agencies and foundations seeking expert counsel on temporary personnel for foreign services.

Related to a comprehensive roster of talent and to the over-all development of the institution's general program is the desirability of utilizing for institutional improvement the available opportunities for individual faculty travel and study and research abroad. While opportunities under the Fulbright program, for example, are handled through institutional nominations, the initiative in such matters almost invariably resides in the individual. The professor who initiates a Fulbright proposal for himself may not be the individual whose work abroad will be of greatest value for the institution's total concerns with international matters. Without diminishing in the least such individual initiative, a policy-making committee may well itself exercise initiative in suggesting nominations to departments or schools or individuals where the university would most profit by having one of its members gain specific foreign experience. The Fulbright awards, or participation in government or foundation enterprises, should be utilized to serve the scholarly interests and aspirations of the institution as well as of individual persons. On this, further discussion will be presented in chapter 5 of this volume.

In making such suggestions as these or in advising on institutional enterprises and developments, the coordinating committee has a responsibility for serving as a clearinghouse of information about available opportunities and resources outside as well as inside the university. One of the major weaknesses in university planning at present is the uncertain way in which many university persons learn of foundation interests, of governmental plans, of research and service opportunities abroad. Some universities have found it useful to maintain offices in Washington; university officials regularly find their way to foundation offices. Both government and foundation officials maintain communication with known individuals, and these should in no sense be reduced. Yet, too frequently, too many institutions or persons who are well qualified to consult on plans as they evolve and capable of participating in their execution learn of the plans too late. Announcements of scholarship awards, of personnel needs abroad, of opportunities for research are very often lost in the intricacies of the campus communication or mailing system. Only an agency continually informed of developments respecting the policies and programs of complex governmental and intergovernmental agencies and foundations with international interests can be alert in evaluating and seizing opportunities for outside resources and service. Only with such knowledge can a coordinating committee and its secretariat adequately serve the different area groups or disciplines or centers which are its constituents within the university.

A well-functioning administrative agency, operating as the secretariat of a comprehensive coordinating committee, would not rest with an inventory of the university's resources and enterprises bearing on international matters and a knowledge of related developments and opportunities outside. Communication of the accumulated information within the academic community is as important as it is ordinarily neglected. Some universities now distribute regularly to all faculty members a roster of foreign visitors. Most university bulletins announce lectures and conferences on international matters. Fragmentary notices on fellowship and research openings are distributed. But more effective instruments for the distribution of information within the university on its international policies, interests, and possibilities are badly needed.

On most large campuses there is probably no one person totally familiar with the international concerns of the whole university, and certainly it is true that most faculty members of every academic community are woefully uninformed of the range and focus and direction of these activities. An important function of a coordinating committee and its secretariat is to make the whole body of faculty and students aware of what is going on. Only by this process can the true "international dimension" of a university take conscious form.

It would be well, therefore, if on each campus there were an annual colloquium for all the faculty members who could be attracted to it, and for representative students, on what the institution is doing or is considering doing under the impact of world affairs. An analysis of the foreign students in the university, prepared by the dean of students, would probably be news, and interesting news, to most faculty members and to the officers of student associations. Reports of foreign enterprises for which departments or schools of the university have contract responsibilities, prospects and summaries of appropriate research studies under way among colleagues, introductions of visiting foreign scholars, recognition of the international prestige of the university's outstanding scholars—a "roundup" of what is going on within the institution covering all such matters could be eminently profitable. It would not only increase the clarity of the university's "international dimension" and stimulate the wider use of resources of talent, but could be an integrating force within the academic community. Too rarely do university faculties thus review, across disciplinary and professional boundaries, such a pervasive, common, and unifying concern.

Of additional importance is the "image" of the university which a well-functioning committee-secretariat may provide for agencies outside the university—for government units, for foundation staff members, for visitors from abroad, and for the public at large. As a channel of communication, such an office may expedite contacts, provide the outsider with a better path to the university units which he is trying to locate, provide a clearer voice for the expression of university policies and positions.

All these organizational and administrative suggestions rest upon assumptions of the inevitability and pervasive scope of the impact of world affairs on higher education. President Pusey has referred to the "irreversible interfusion of American and world affairs." There is likewise an "irreversible interfusion" of academic concerns and international statecraft. This is evident among nations throughout the contemporary world and is perhaps particularly striking in the United States where a pragmatic tradition has always tended to minimize separation of learning and life. The important point is, to quote President Pusey again, that under the emerging circumstances of widened cultural contacts and intellectual interests among nations, universities must develop "a conception of their task commensurate with national responsibilities which are now world wide."

4

Governmental Programs of International Cultural Relations

No clearer indication of the pervasive influence of world affairs on American colleges and universities can be found than is revealed by surveying even briefly the national programs of international cultural relations on which the government of the United States has, in recent decades, embarked. A wide variety of federal programs in education, science, and culture which have been developed in the interests of foreign policy or of national security, embody both responsibilities and opportunities for American institutions of higher education. The interrelations between government and universities in respect to these programs are complex and provide full evidence of the necessity for long-range academic policy on the part of every institution touched by them.

Federal Activities in Cultural Relations before 1946

Formally, the United States was a latecomer to the field of governmental cultural relations with other nations, though the roots of such programs reach deeply into the American tradition. Exchange of publications between the Library of Congress and foreign libraries was authorized as early as 1840. The Smithsonian Institution began distribution of its publications abroad in 1849. In 1896 the federal Bureau of Education was made responsible for preparing and publishing studies of the educational practices and policies of other countries. Since 1908 the Pan American

Union, now the Secretariat of the Organization of American States, has, with the United States as a supporting member, facilitated the hemispheric exchange of publications and persons. In 1908 an epochal binational agreement, precursor of the Fulbright exchanges, was negotiated between the United States and China, by which the $18 million Boxer indemnity fund was set up as a special foundation for the "promotion of education and culture." This fund subsequently financed the education of more than 3,000 Chinese students in American colleges and universities. Following World War I, unexpended funds of the Belgian War Relief Commission were set up as the Belgian-American Foundation for the support of a binational exchange of students and scholars. Participation in such agencies as the International Postal Union, representation in a series of world fairs as cultural and trade events, occasional financial support for representation at international scientific and cultural conferences—all indicated a rising degree of governmental involvement in cultural matters as the United States moved into the first decades of the twentieth century. Although the United States did not participate in the work of the International Institute of Intellectual Cooperation under the League of Nations, a group of influential Americans organized a National Committee on Intellectual Cooperation which maintained close contact with the international agency.

Almost unconsciously, the United States was developing, along with all other major states, cultural elements within its foreign policy. Part of the motivation for this trend was political and in some degree propagandistic; the two World Wars witnessed the establishment of enormous information services by virtually every nation, and these were continued into postwar years of uncertain peace as instruments for creating understanding of the country abroad. But there were additional motivations, deep-rooted in the desire to attain a more perfect civilization. Learned and cultured men in all countries felt it worthwhile to encourage cultural interchange as a value in itself. By the 1930's the United

States found it desirable both to increase its information services abroad and to facilitate the cultural activities of international scope in which so many of its own citizens, as well as citizens of other countries, were interested. At the end of the depression decade, in the lull before World War II, the government took the first tentative steps in formulating a basic, comprehensive, and long-range policy on the role of cultural affairs in foreign policy and international relations.

During the late 1930's three developments occurred which are landmarks in the rise of American interest in this field. In 1936 the Inter-American Conference for the Maintenance of Peace, meeting in Buenos Aires, produced a Convention for the Promotion of Inter-American Cultural Relations. Though it favored the objectives of the convention, the United States delegation opposed it on the ground that the Federal Government had no authority over educational matters. Two years later, however, the government ratified the convention, though with cautious reservations about its power in certain fields. The convention led to enormously increased activities in the cultural implementation by American agencies, public and private, of the "good neighbor" policy. In 1938, also, the Federal Government, seeking to encourage and coordinate these activities, created an Interdepartmental Committee on Scientific and Cultural Cooperation. The signing of the Inter-American cultural agreement and the establishment of the interdepartmental committee made 1938 an important year in the history of our international relations.

Of even greater consequence was the establishment under Cordell Hull, also in 1938, of an office of cultural relations within the Department of State. Before setting up the office, the Department invited leaders in education, science, communications, and the arts to a series of consultations. In these it was agreed that (1) cultural relations between nations should be reciprocal, (2) in such relations, so far as the United States was concerned, nongovernmental groups and private citizens should share responsibility and action along with the government, and (3) programs should be objective in their presentation of America abroad. The line between propaganda—even objective information-giving—and cultural relations must be as clearly drawn as possible. By the departmental order creating it, the new Division of Cultural Relations was charged with

> the exchange of professors, teachers, and students; cooperation in the fields of music, art, literature, and other cultural and intellectual attainments; the formulation and distribution of libraries of representative works on the United States, and suitable translations thereof; the participation by this government in international radio broadcasts; encouragement of closer relations between unofficial organizations of this and of foreign governments engaged in cultural and intellectual activities; and, generally, the dissemination abroad of the representative intellectual and cultural works of the United States and the improvement and broadening of the scope of our cultural relations with other countries.[1]

The newly established division was inevitably regarded with mixed feelings by the "old hands" of the Department of State. Inevitably, too, it was engaged in a complex mixture of information activities for political ends and "cultural and intellectual" activities of common international concern. And it was from the outset involved in the problems of coordination between public and private sectors of activity. Warmly supported, however, by the Secretary, and ably led by Ben Cherrington, on leave from the Social Science Foundation at Denver, the Division opened up paths of mounting scope and consequence. It administered grants for the exchange of students and professors as provided for in the Convention for the Promotion of Inter-American Cultural Relations. Relying heavily upon educational institutions and such organizations as the American Council on Education, it stimulated foreign and international studies, the improvement of our treatment of Latin America in school and college teaching materials, and the development of scholarships from private sources for foreign students.

[1] State Department, *Departmental Order No. 367*, July 27, 1938.

The early advent of World War II both increased the work of the division and brought into existence a variety of other governmental agencies, such as the more heavily financed Office of the Coordinator of Inter-American Affairs under Nelson Rockefeller and the Office of War Information under Elmer Davis. In the rapid, urgent developments of the war years, distinctions between political and scholarly motivations were blurred, overlapping of functions among a variety of governmental units was accelerated, a wide range of activities was developed without long-range policy authorizations by the Congress. By the end of the war, even without over-all policy and planning, the United States was more deeply involved than ever in many informational, educational, scientific, and cultural relations with other nations. Moreover, the increased prestige and power of the United States inevitably made American cultural characteristics of greater concern to other countries. And, in the postwar years, as had been emphasized, the cultural ingredients of international relations took on a more vital role in foreign policy for all nations. United States activities in 1945 were in some ways disorganized at the administrative level, more a patchwork of hastily put together items than a long-range program, without basic legislative structuring on anything wider than the prewar hemispheric level. The war years both increased the importance of cultural relations and the complexities of developing a balanced, long-range policy.

The Fulbright and Smith-Mundt Acts

The postwar decade brought significant new programs at the same time that it witnessed a sequence of administrative reorganizations. A series of bills passed by the Congress after 1945 added new strength and new dimensions to the total cultural enterprise. The first of these was the amendment to the War Surplus Property Act proposed by Senator J. William Fulbright, passed by Congress, and signed by President Truman on August 1, 1946.[2] This imaginative legislation, which has since made the

[2] Public Law 584, 79th Congress.

term "Fulbright" synonymous with a scholarly exchange fellowship and has affected almost every campus in the United States, provided that funds derived from the sale abroad of war surplus property might be used, under terms of mutual agreement with the purchasing countries, to "finance studies, research, instruction, and other educational activities." A ten-member Board of Foreign Scholarships, composed largely of academic persons, was set up to supervise the Fulbright program in the United States. In each cooperating country a Fulbright Commission, composed of citizens of the United States resident in that country together with an equal number of its nationals, was established.

The network of Fulbright Commissions all over the world, closely related to the Board of Foreign Scholarships in the United States, has become a major factor in the cultural relations of contemporary nations. Using the currencies of other countries, steadily extending its financial base beyond that involved in the sale of war surplus properties and its geographic coverage beyond the nation-purchasers of such properties, the Fulbright program, in 1961, operated actively in 40 countries, with a total budget of approximately $14.6 million. In that year, the program brought 2,493 persons to the United States, and sent 1,679 American scholars abroad. By 1962, a total of 19,507 Americans had gone abroad on Fulbright grants to lecture or teach or conduct research, and 31,319 young foreign scholars had been aided in an American educational experience in this country or in an American-sponsored school abroad. The Fulbright program had, in effect, become a permanent part of American foreign policy.

Within the United States elaborate procedures were set up for selecting Fulbright candidates, involving regional review committees, and all colleges and universities. The principle laid down in the 1930's of involving nongovernmental agencies intimately in the exchange programs was adhered to. The Institute of International Education, privately established soon after World War I, was designated as the agency to handle predoctoral awards under the Fulbright program. Heaviest emphasis, however, was placed on postdoctoral awards. A joint committee—the Conference Board of Associated Research Councils—representing the Social Science Research Council, the National Science Foundation, the American Council of Learned Societies, and the American Council on Education was formed to handle postdoctoral grants. This joint committee, with a secretariat headed by Dr. Francis Young, has been the chief operational agent in the Fulbright exchanges and represents a significant and successful instance of academic-governmental cooperation. One of the activities of the Conference Board was development during the 1950's of a series of regional conferences for Fulbright scholars visiting the United States. At these conferences the nature of American higher education was explored. Reports from the conferences, available through the Conference Board, constitute a useful body of literature with particular reference to comparative studies in higher education.

A year and a half after the enactment of the Fulbright Act, the United States Information and Educational Act of 1948 was passed by Congress.[3] Sponsored by Senator H. Alexander Smith and Representative (later Senator) Karl E. Mundt, the act authorized the Department of State to set up a cultural and information program on a global basis. With the objective of promoting a better understanding of the United States in other countries and of increasing mutual understanding between the people of the United States and the people of other countries, the Smith-Mundt Act provided congressional authorization for broad cultural activities on a global scale. It provided for "an information service to disseminate abroad information about the United States . . . [and] an educational exchange service to cooperate with other nations in the interchange of persons, knowledge, and skills." It set up an Advisory Committee on Information and an Advisory Commission on Educational Exchange. The act stipulated that the Department of State should make use wherever

[3] Public Law 402, 80th Congress.

possible of "reputable private agencies" in carrying out the educational exchange program. For this program, the dollar funds made available in successive federal budgets have complemented the foreign currencies made available for the support of exchange under the Fulbright Act. Under the Smith-Mundt Act, the United States Information Service (USIS) was established, as well as the Office of Educational Exchange, which in 1952 became the International Educational Exchange Service (IES). In 1953 the information services were moved out of the Department of State and set up as the United States Information Agency (USIA), known abroad as the United States Information Service (USIS). USIA provides aid in such activities as securing American lecturers abroad, promoting the teaching of English, establishing and maintaining American libraries all over the world, and promoting American studies in foreign universities.

AID and Its Precursors

From the pronouncement of a Point Four Program in President Truman's inaugural address of 1949 came a series of legislative acts and executive orders [4] which produced the International Cooperation Administration as a semiautonomous agency in the Department of State. The purpose of the programs developed by the International Cooperation Administration (ICA) and its predecessor organizations was basically the cultivation of viable economies and cultures and political systems in newly emerging, relatively underdeveloped states. At first the development projects were largely technical—construction of highways and airports, development of electrical power resources, establishment

[4] Economic Cooperation Act of 1948 (62 Stat. 138), amended 1949 (63 Stat. 50) and 1950 (64 Stat. 198); Mutual Security Act of 1951 (65 Stat. 373); Mutual Security Act of 1952 (66 Stat. 141); Foreign Operations Administration, President's Reorganization Plan 7 and Executive Order 10476 of August 1, 1953; Mutual Security Act of 1954 (68 Stat. 832); Executive Order 10610 of May 9, 1955; Foreign Assistance Act of 1961 (75 Stat. 445) and Executive Order 10973 of Nov. 3, 1961.

of industries. But with these matters came increasing concern with the development of human resources, involving not only technical training but also broader general education as a basic quality in manpower training. Health projects, social service enterprises, and development of schools and colleges gradually took on major importance in the ICA programs. "Institution building," by which a new nation might cultivate its own resources and train its own manpower, became the focus of attention. By 1961, when the International Cooperation Administration was reorganized as the Agency for International Development (AID), the programs carried on under its authority were of direct concern to the academic world, involving matters ranging from general to specialized education, from the sciences, both natural and social, to the applications of learning in all phases of development.

The enormous expansion of ICA–AID activities under the impetus of emerging nations in Asia and Africa as well as the course of the cold war, led to heavy emphasis on development enterprises in the national activities of international cultural relations. Cultural programs tended increasingly to be formulated in terms of the needs and requests of the relatively new, relatively underindustrialized nations. Large numbers of federal employees drawn from professional and scholarly fields were placed in federal service abroad, as the overseas staff of ICA–AID increased.

Not only academic personnel but universities themselves were soon drawn into the operations of foreign developmental programs. In 1951, the first Director of the Technical Cooperation Administration began a system of university contracts which has proved to be one of the best techniques in developmental operations. By 1959 some 53 United States universities were operating educational programs in 33 countries under contract with ICA. In April 1962 the number of projects of this character had increased to 103, involving 62 universities working in 57 countries and areas of the world. Under contracts in this program, for example, Harvard and UCLA are aiding Nigeria in the establishment of two model comprehensive high schools; the University of Nebraska is cooperating in the development of a land-grant university in Turkey; Indiana University is developing audio-visual educational programs abroad. American schools of engineering, of education, of public health, of public administration, of library science, and of agriculture are involved in direct cooperation, under United States sponsorship, with educational institutions and public enterprises around the world. While the development of the university contract system did not occur without controversy and moments of agonizing reappraisal, the system has steadily improved. A series of conferences convened by the American Council on Education were instrumental in this improvement.

The development of foreign aid programs is, of course, obviously closely related to foreign policy and to political movements. The Agency for International Development and its precursor organizations have been among the most difficult of the federal agencies to administer; even the university contract system has on occasion bogged down in a bureaucratic tangle or found it almost impossible to discover the effective mixture of cultural elements, humanitarian motivations, financial limitations, and lines of political policy. A succession of administrative reorganizations has taken place, and there has been a mounting effort to determine an efficient degree of long-range planning in the program. In 1962 a new Director of the agency, David Bell, was appointed, and a high-level committee headed by General Lucius Clay was set up to study the agency and to formulate recommendations for its further development. The recommendations suggest administrative and planning changes, greater focus on selected countries, and elimination of certain wastages, but, in total, strongly support the continuation of the program.

The Fulbright exchanges, the Smith-Mundt programs, the Information Services, and the AID programs are by no means the only federal enterprises abroad in fields that are of direct concern to American colleges and universities. Almost every executive department and many special agencies—the Atomic Energy Commission, the Library of Congress, the Tennessee Valley Authority, the National Science Foundation, to name only a few—carry on international and foreign programs which have academic relevance. These activities range in character and scope from the acceptance of a small foreign group for technical training to a very large program for the education of military personnel, from the short-term visits of foreign leaders to cooperative ventures in basic research, from the establishment of American libraries abroad to the reception of artists and exhibits on American tour from other countries.

A detailed description of the international educational programs carried on by some twenty departments and agencies of the Federal Government is available,[5] and need not be elaborated here. Certain illustrations of government activity, in addition to those already described, should be given. The Office of Education, in the Department of Health, Education, and Welfare, is an example. It has an international program of its own and is also the operative agent for certain activities sponsored by other governmental units; it works in close relation with schools and institutions of higher education throughout the country.

The United States Office of Education

One of the three operational units of the Office of Education[6] is the Bureau of International Education. The Bureau is composed of two divisions, one conducting international education studies and the other dealing with technical assistance and exchange programs. Among the programs administered by these divisions,

[5] *Government Programs in International Education (A Survey and Handbook), Forty-second Report by the Committee on Government Operations,* House Report No. 2712, 85th Cong., 2d Sess. (Washington: Government Printing Office, 1959).

[6] "Organization Guide, Office of Education," May 1, 1962. Multilithed.

ordinarily under direct contract with the Department of State and involving institutional cooperation, are:

1. The *International Teacher Development Program,* by which more than 4,500 teachers, administrators, and ministry officials from 83 countries and territories have been brought to the United States since 1944. Recipients of grants under this program combine periods of study in colleges and universities with extensive observation of American education.

2. The *Teacher Exchange Program,* by which direct interchange of teaching positions with counterparts abroad has been arranged for 2,277 American teachers since 1946; 1,182 additional American teachers have been enabled to teach abroad without interchange for a year since 1949; 240 foreign teachers have been brought to the United States for a year of teaching; 864 Americans have gone abroad for summer seminars since 1952; and, since 1958, 80 school administrators have been sent abroad for comparative education seminars. The Teacher Exchange program, beginning with Great Britain in 1946, now operates in cooperation with 67 countries and territories.

3. The *Technical Assistance Training Program.* In 1951, the Office of Education was requested by the Technical Cooperation Administration (now AID) to arrange for the training in the United States of nine persons brought from three countries. By 1961 this program had arranged training (given by 245 colleges, universities, trade schools, and technical institutes) for 3,026 participants from 69 countries. In 1962 an additional 850 were cared for.

In these programs, and others like them, the Office of Education becomes the administering agency for enterprises developed by units within the Department of State. But in terms of its own authorized functions, the Office also (1) conducts, coordinates, and contracts for analytical research studies on foreign educational systems, (2) collects, summarizes, and reports on official educational documents from abroad, (3) analyzes, on request, the credentials and academic transcripts of students coming from abroad, (4) maintains an active program in comparative education, (5) collects information about the understanding abroad of American education, (6) maintains a collection of curricula, textbooks, and educational documents from other countries, and (7) publishes statistical and interpretative data on foreign educational developments for use by American educators. It works closely with American educational organizations and institutions in developing American policy toward educational programs of international organizations. Indeed, so extensive have become the Office's responsibilities in the development of education as a factor in foreign policy that it is sometimes attacked, though unjustly, by rightist organizations as an agency of foreign influences.

A new dimension was added to the work of the Office of Education by the National Defense Education Act, passed by Congress in 1958.[7] The act authorizes a series of domestic educational activities which derive their impetus from international concerns. Enacted as a reaction to Sputnik I, it emphasizes educational improvement at points particularly related to our defense posture. Although based by no means on a thoroughly conceived policy respecting federal responsibilities in education, it has provided significant federal financial aid in a number of important academic areas and activities.

The act embodies ten titles. The first recognizes that "we must increase our efforts to identify and educate more of the talent of our nation" and that we must correct imbalances by intensifying education "in science, mathematics, foreign languages, and ... technology." The second title then provides for loans to college and university students; under this title the Federal Government had provided approximately $202 million to 1,468 institutions of higher education up to June 30, 1962. Studies indicate that the funds were drawing into the universities many worthy students

[7] Public Law 158, 86th Congress.

who would not otherwise be there, or who would be studying on a part-time rather than a full-time basis. The grants, administered with care by institutions, substantially aided in their recruitment of talent.

Title III provides "financial assistance for strengthening Science, Mathematics, and Foreign Language Instruction." Seventy million dollars for each of the four years of the Act are provided for the purchase of needed science equipment in schools, with additional funds for providing more effective supervision for instruction in science, mathematics, and languages from state departments of education. Improved teaching under these activities is already producing better-prepared entrants for college work. Title IV provides National Defense Fellowships for graduate study in areas of particular importance. By 1963–64 approximately 5,500 such fellowships will have been granted, each for three years of graduate, degree-focused study. NDEA Fellowships from this source are now a familiar element in university graduate schools, and have strengthened markedly many programs for comprehensive study of world areas.

The cultivation of talent is particularly dependent upon effective counseling and guidance services in schools and colleges. Title V authorizes the expenditure of $15 million a year for four years in grants to state educational agencies for better guidance programs, including testing and counseling. Title VI provides for the development of university centers for the study of previously neglected languages, research on linguistics and language instruction, and the training of language teachers for the schools. Under this program, academic offerings and research in the language fields have become increasingly prominent in American academic planning, and registrations in language courses have markedly increased. Title VII concerns itself with research and experimentation in the educational use of mass media and newer technological tools of instruction, an area of increasing concern to higher education. Title VIII supports vocational programs important to the national defense. Title IX provides for the dissemination of scientific information. Title X increases the financial support for statistical services of state educational agencies.

Altogether, the programs supported under the National Defense Education Act have strengthened American education at all levels, and have in particular influenced the programs of instruction, research, and service in colleges and universities. The act of 1958 continued in effect for four years, and has now been extended to 1964. In some form, it seems likely to become relatively permanent. Certain crash aspects of the program may well be reduced, but provision for loans, fellowships, and the support of academic programs falling within the range of the act may advantageously be increased. It is likely, too, that the social sciences have a deeper pertinence to civic vitality and therefore to national defense than was recognized in 1958. Certainly in the revision and extension of the act, colleges and universities have a major interest.

The National Science Foundation

Although most of the titles of the National Defense Education Act are administered through the Office of Education, some are administered through the National Science Foundation, and the entire program is closely related to the work of the Foundation. The Foundation, established by congressional act in 1950 as an independent agency of the Federal Government to promote scientific progress, has been and is one of the most significant avenues of communication and influence between government and higher education. For fiscal year 1961 close to $176,500,000 was available to the Foundation for the support of (1) basic scientific research, (2) increase in research facilities, (3) programs for improving course content and for assisting science teachers, students, and advanced scholars, and (4) programs for increasing the availability of research results. Its 4,196 fellowship awardees were to be found in 190 institutions in the United States and 70 institutions abroad.

Although the resources of the National Science Foundation are primarily devoted to support of basic scientific research in the United States, such Foundation activities as its grants for the translation of foreign scientific literature and support of research in mechanical translation and linguistic analysis markedly facilitate international communication in the sciences and related fields of knowledge. Included in the organizational structure of the Foundation is an Office of International Science Activities. This office is responsible for initiating and developing cooperative and experimental programs in international science and science education, for liaison with other government agencies involved in such activities, and for providing backstopping service in support of United States participation in selected international organizations such as Unesco.

The Mutual Educational and Cultural Exchange Act of 1961

Fifteen years after the passage of the Fulbright Act, so great a variety of legislative items dealt directly or indirectly with cultural relations abroad, that some codification of them was urgent. In 1961 a Mutual Educational and Cultural Exchange Act,[8] widely known as the Fulbright-Hays Act, was passed by the Congress. The purpose of the act is

> to enable the Government of the United States to increase mutual understanding between the people of the United States and the people of other countries by means of educational and cultural exchange; to strengthen the ties which unite us with other nations by demonstrating the educational and cultural interests, developments, and achievements of the people of the United States and other nations, and the contributions being made toward a peaceful and more fruitful life for people throughout the world; to promote international cooperation for educational and cultural advancement; and thus to assist in the development of friendly, sympathetic, and peaceful relations between the United States and the other countries of the world.

[8] Public Law 256, Sept. 21, 1961, 87th Congress.

The act authorizes educational exchanges "by financing studies, research, instruction, and other educational activities" for American citizens going abroad or for citizens of other countries coming to the United States. It authorizes the financing of cultural exchanges, including grants for leaders and experts, tours of "artists and athletes," and United States representation in meetings and festivals abroad. It authorizes (1) interchanges of books, instructional materials, and research instruments, (2) the establishment of cultural centers, (3) assistance to educational institutions abroad, (4) cultivation of American studies abroad, (5) promotion of medical, scientific, cultural and educational research and development, (6) representation at international conferences, and (7) "independent research into the problems of educational and cultural exchange." It authorizes the negotiation of binational and multinational cultural agreements, the employment and training of necessary personnel, the making of grants-in-aid. It brings into relationship the various financial resources for support of the cultural relations program.

While many of the fundamental features of the act of 1961 are restatements of earlier legislation, there are several important innovations. For the first time, orientation and counseling services maintained by the government are available to all foreign students rather than only to foreign students here under government grants. The act provides the first general authority for direct federal support of such institutions of cultural exchange as the East-West Center in Hawaii. The law expands authority to support programs in American studies in foreign universities. For the first time assistance is specifically authorized for financial support of representation at nongovernmental international conferences of an educational, scientific, and technical character, including festivals and competitions. The authority to support research and development pertaining to international educational and cultural affairs is amplified and provision made for the more flexible use of federal funds.

The United States Advisory Committee on Educational Exchange is replaced by a nine-member Advisory Commission on International and Cultural Affairs. The Commission

> shall formulate and recommend to the President policies for exercising his authority under this Act and shall appraise the effectiveness of programs carried out pursuant to it. The Commission shall make a special study of past programs.

In May 1962 the members of the Commission were appointed,[9] with John Gardner as its chairman. It has already launched a survey and appraisal of American experience in the international cultural field, and has dealt with specific policy problems put before it by the Assistant Secretary of State for Cultural Affairs. The Commission, small enough to be readily accessible, representative of the nation's cultural interests, free from administrative and supervisory responsibilities, may well become the chief policy-recommending agency for the government in its field. It must, however, be supplemented by nongovernmental agencies of an equally high-level and effective character.

The 1961 act increases the Board of Foreign Scholarships from ten to twelve members and extends its counseling responsibilities to cover a wider range of academic exchangees. It continues also a special Advisory Committee on the Arts, originally established in 1956, and authorizes the President to establish such additional interagency and advisory committees as may seem desirable.

The United States in Unesco

In 1946 the United States ratified the Charter of the United Nations Educational, Scientific, and Cultural Organization, be-

[9] The members are: John W. Gardner (chairman), president of the Carnegie Corporation of New York; Walter Adams, professor of economics, Michigan State University; James R. Fleming, publisher, *Fort Wayne* (Indiana) *Journal-Gazette;* Luther Hilton Foster, president, Tuskegee Institute; Reverend Theodore M. Hesburgh, president, University of Notre Dame; Walter Johnson, chairman, Department of History, University of Chicago; Roy E. Larson, chairman, Executive Committee, Time Incorporated; Franklin D. Murphy, chancellor, University of California, Los Angeles; Mrs. Mabel M. Smith, principal, New Lincoln High School, New York.

coming one of its founding member states. Unesco, one of the specialized agencies of the United Nations, has steadily expanded its operations in the international field since its establishment, and throughout its career the United States has been active in its councils and enterprises.

The Unesco program, determined by a biennial General Conference composed of delegates from member states, is operated through a group of secretariat departments. Its Department of Education has developed a program of yearbooks devoted to educational statistics, has stimulated widespread attacks on illiteracy, has established centers for child study, has encouraged regional planning for educational development, has encouraged new approaches in comparative education. The Department of Natural Sciences has fostered scientific research, aided scientific associations, initiated the International Geophysical Year, studied the problems of arid lands, and begun an appraisal of food resources in the oceans. The Department of Social Sciences has stimulated the establishment of international scholarly organizations in its field. The Department of Cultural Relations has facilitated artistic exchanges, translations of classics, and reproductions of art works. Through conferences, committees of experts, special seminars, field services, publications, the drafting of international agreements, and by other techniques Unesco has added an international voice to the cultural conversations among nations.[10]

Unesco is related to the United States through the Department of State and by a United States National Commission for Unesco, which was authorized by Congress in the act of ratification of the Unesco constitution. The Commission is a unique political invention, composed of one hundred members, three-fifths of whom are selected as their representatives by national organizations. It has the responsibility for advising the Secretary of State on all

[10] See Walter H. C. Laves and Charles A. Thompson, *Unesco: Purpose, Progress, Prospects* (Bloomington: Indiana University Press, 1957), xxiii + 469 pp.

Unesco matters; the Commission secretariat is a unit within the Department of State. The Commission, through its committees, also takes the initiative in arranging for participation in Unesco-sponsored projects by United States organizations and institutions. In a sense the Commission both speaks to the government and speaks to the citizenry on Unesco and Unesco-related matters. It is required by law to sponsor every other year a national conference on some aspect of international cultural relations. In recent years these conferences, devoted to American cultural relations with such world areas as Africa, Latin America, and the European community, have become important opinion-making events bringing together organizational and institutional leaders from all over the nation. The precise role and significance of the National Commission, however, has yet to be determined. Too large to be an effective advisory body, with a rotating membership, with limited financing, the Commission has not realized the hopes of its creators. It is now highly desirable to coordinate it more effectively with the commissions which have been established under the Fulbright-Hays Act of 1961.

In many respects, Unesco has been a center of controversy in the United States. Originally overestimated by many devotees of international understanding as an influential force, Unesco has sought to determine its most effective role through trial and error, and its mistakes have sometimes been overemphasized. In general, the United States has tended to look upon Unesco as primarily a philanthropic agency; its early activities in educational relief and rehabilitation and its later emphasis on aid to underdeveloped areas have contributed to this concept. More recently, however, there has been a legitimate concern with what value the Unesco program has for the United States. With attention to enlightened self-interest, the United States participation in Unesco enterprises, the coordination of its work with other international agencies and with binational programs, and an increase in its efficiency as a growing organization have been the concern of the United States.

Binational Cultural Conventions

While Great Britain, France, and other European nations have entered into a complex of binational cultural conventions, the United States has not done so, primarily because the role of the Federal Government in such relations was not clear. But the United States has recently made a start in that direction, for after a protracted period of difficulties in relations between the Union of Soviet Socialist Republics and the United States, the governments of the two countries authorized negotiations which began in late 1957 and resulted in January 1958 in an Exchange Agreement. This bilateral convention is now an important, even though difficult and sometimes disappointing, element in our cultural relations policy.

Designed to open up cultural channels between the two countries, the agreement authorized exchanges in the "cultural, technical and educational fields." Basic arrangements for exchanges of radio and television broadcasts; of specialists in industry, agriculture, and medicine; of cultural, civic, youth and student groups; of parliamentary delegations; of scientists; of theatrical, choral, and choreographic groups, symphony orchestras, and artistic performers; of athletes and sports teams; of university delegations; and of exhibits and publications were outlined in the convention. While many problems plagued the development of some of the exchanges, the program on the whole has been an asset to both countries. The agreement was renewed and, in some ways, expanded in 1962.

It seems desirable that the United States should extend its bilateral cultural relations programs by further development of specific cultural agreements. An agreement between Canada and the United States is in many ways desirable. During World War II the Carnegie Endowment for International Peace took the initiative in organizing a nongovernmental Canadian-American Committee on Education, with members representing educational organizations in the two countries. The committee, with joint chairmen and secretaries, made surveys of how each country was treated in the school textbooks of the other; prepared the only comprehensive catalogue of educational exchanges between the two countries; examined some of the perplexing questions of interchange of books, magazines, teaching materials, films, and radio programs; and prepared statements about the relations of the two countries appropriate for school curricula. The committee did an excellent job with the meager resources it had available, but it has now passed out of existence. While the basic relations of the two countries are excellent, there continue to be certain frustrations of interchange and lack of complete understanding. In order to maintain the best relations between the two countries, a basic core of cultural relations should be guaranteed by the governments, and a channel of continuing communication through a responsible binational committee on educational and cultural relations should be established. Such a committee could function effectively as a study group devoted to prevention of misunderstanding.

Even more complex is the problem of our educational relations with Mexico. The relations between the organized education groups of the two countries are currently at low ebb. It would be advantageous to explore fully the possibility of sustaining educational and cultural relations between the two neighbors by an active program specifically outlined in a formal agreement.

The Bureau of Cultural Affairs

Twenty-three years after Ben Cherrington became the first cultural relations officer of the Department of State, the Department created a special Bureau of Cultural Affairs and put at its head an Assistant Secretary of State for Cultural Affairs. The first Assistant Secretary was Philip Coombs; he was succeeded by Lucius D. Battle. These two men set the pattern of organization by which the government recognized as never before cultural matters as a new dimension in foreign policy and international affairs.

The Bureau, headed by the Assistant Secretary, includes the

staffs which service the advisory committees already referred to —the secretariats for the United States National Commission for Unesco, the United States Commission on International Educational and Cultural Affairs, the Advisory Committee on the Arts, and the Board of Foreign Scholarships. In order to coordinate the operations of these committees, of the divers specialized agencies of the United Nations, of United States action in connection with such regional agencies as the Organization of American States, and with binational programs, the Bureau is organized under a series of area officers comparable to the political area desks of the Department of State. Thus, chief cultural relations officers are established to deal, respectively, with Inter-American programs, Far Eastern programs, African programs, European programs, and Near Eastern and South Asian programs. Units within the Bureau deal with the often vexatious questions of cultural presentations abroad and with programs and services within the United States.

The establishment and organization of the Bureau with the status given it in the Department—a status requisite to the recruitment of an effective staff—mark a new level of maturity in American cultural operations in the international field. The dimension of cultural affairs in foreign policy is recognized and the dimension is more effectively related to the traditional political and economic aspects of diplomacy. The Bureau facilitates more effective communication between the government and the cultural, scientific, and educational forces of American life, including its institutions of higher education.

The Peace Corps

One of the most recent and dramatic developments in the cultural aspects of American foreign policy is the Peace Corps. Rooted in the deep desire of many individuals to make a direct, personal, active contribution to social improvement, the Peace Corps provides something of the challenge and satisfaction of which William James wrote in "The Moral Equivalent to War." Certainly the concepts and motivations of the Corps are not recent phenomena in human experience. Religious institutions, philanthropic organizations, and youth groups have long cultivated opportunities and enterprises for direct service, often in foreign lands. Many agencies such as the American Friends Service Committee developed notable "youth work camps" in connection with the rehabilitation of areas devastated in World War II. In recent years, a group of church denominations in the United States, cooperating through an agency called International Voluntary Services, sometimes aided by ICA funds, have sent several hundred young volunteers to work on service projects in newly developing nations. Australia early sent young men and women on volunteer service in Southeast Asia. Various United Nations agencies have utilized volunteers in worthy enterprises, recruited on a multinational basis.

All of these experiences and their animating ideas have been crystallized in the United States Peace Corps. In January 1960, Senator Richard Neuberger and Representative Henry Reuss introduced into Congress a bill, incorporated into the ICA Appropriations Act, which provided $10,000 for "a study of the advisability and practicability of a Point Four Youth Corps." In the same session, Senator Hubert Humphrey introduced a bill for the establishment of a "United States Peace Corps." During the presidental campaign of 1960, Senator John F. Kennedy mentioned Peace Corps development at an informal meeting with students at the University of Michigan and found such an enthusiastic reception for the idea that he elaborated on it at a later speech in San Francisco. The proposal quickly won national attention and provoked lively debate. After his inauguration as President, he established the Peace Corps on a temporary, pilot basis by Executive order on March 1, 1961, and asked Congress to enact legislation to make the Corps permanent. At first the action was received with mixed and partisan feelings, but the Peace Corps has steadily won increasing public and governmental support. With a $30 million budget in its trial year, the Corps was allotted by Congress $59 million for its second year. There is strong indication that the Peace Corps will be an enduring and long-range instrument of American foreign policy, not only because it provides a service well received in developing countries, but also because it provides a satisfying and educative experience useful to many American citizens.

Within seven months after its establishment the Peace Corps had dispatched its first group of volunteers—31 surveyors, geologists, and engineers to Tanganyika for assignment to a road building enterprise—and had sent a group of 50 men and women as teachers in Ghana. By the end of its first year, the Corps had 698 volunteers in the field. Forty-five volunteers were working on community development projects in Chile and 62 in similar enterprises in Colombia; 26 volunteers were helping in agricultural programs in India; 182 were serving as teacher aids in the Philippines; 107 were teaching in Nigerian secondary schools. The Director of the Peace Corps, Sargent Shriver, could report that on March 1, 1963, when the Corps was two years old, it had 4,008 volunteers at work in 41 countries. Negotiations for expansion into other countries were under way, and the Corps activities of recruitment and selection, training, and placement were stepped up steadily in succeeding months.

At the outset, the Peace Corps was popularly, though mistakenly, conceived as purely a youth corps. Though, of course, the great majority of volunteers are and will continue to be men and women in their twenties and thirties (the average age is 26), there are over two dozen volunteers serving overseas who are in their sixties. The Corps does have special appeal for the young, and is most feasible for many individuals in the years just after graduation from college or university. But it is really a service group calling for specific training and skills, ordinarily at professional and semiprofessional levels, in its recruits. The skills are by no means limited to the young nor are the motivations to service so limited. Each year a somewhat larger number of older people, particularly among the groups volunteering for teaching, has been recruited. This tendency may be furthered by the fact that an increasing number of American school systems are putting into effect arrangements by which experienced teachers on their staffs may be released for tours of duty with the Peace Corps or on other foreign assignment without loss of tenure, promotion, or retirement privileges.

The Peace Corps has contracted with a considerable number of American colleges and universities to train volunteers. While its contract operations of this character have not yet been as well developed as the university contracts of AID and have been harassed by the speed with which the program has developed, it seems logical that colleges and universities should be brought into closer relationship with the Peace Corps in recruiting, selecting, training, screening, placing, and supervising people in the field. Peace Corps service is itself an educative experience which needs to be integrated more closely with the total training experience of young professionals. In such fields as engineering, agriculture, health, and education, much of the preparation for Peace Corps assignments could be built into a university's regular program of instructing, with Peace Corps service as a type of field internship, and with such service planned as preparatory to further university training after completion of a tour of duty. The ultimate development of the Peace Corps is likely to bring government and universities into increased cooperation in facilitating planned careers for individual volunteers.

New Types of Institutions

Governmental needs and policies and programs, as has been indicated throughout this volume, have markedly influenced developments in academic institutions. They have encouraged the kinds of organizational adjustments described in chapter 3. In addition, under the impact of world affairs, there have been various proposals for the development of new academic institutions, sometimes directly under the auspices of the government itself. At times suggestions have been put forward for the establishment of a new national university exclusively for foreign students, but the proposals have received little support. The experience of the Soviet Union with the People's Friendship University for foreign students seems generally unsuccessful.

A proposal presently before the Congress for establishment of a National Academy of Foreign Affairs seems better considered and more widely supported. The proposed academy is unlike the military service academies already maintained by the government; it is envisaged as a professional school on the graduate level for career officers in the Foreign Service and other government employees stationed abroad. In one sense it is more like the War College; it is not expected to grant degrees but to provide instruction designed to update and upgrade personnel directly involved in international relations. It could function also as a major research center in the continuing analysis of international programs. Recommended by a special Presidential advisory committee under the chairmanship of James A. Perkins, formerly of the Carnegie Corporation and now president of Cornell, plans for the new academy are embodied in legislation proposed by Senator Symington.

A new institution, federally financed and already in operation, is the Center for Cultural and Technical Interchange Between East and West—usually called the East-West Center, located in Honolulu. After considerable organizational confusion in its early months, the center is now launched on a program of major consequence. The center is located on the campus of the University of Hawaii, with programs which take full advantage of its location at "the crossroads of the Pacific." At the center a series of international seminars are held, dealing with aspects of cultural relations between Occident and Orient. Research materials appropriate for its program are being rapidly accumulated at the center. An East-West Center Press is being established, as well as a translation center for the facilitation of research. A particularly imaginative element in the center's program is provision for scholars-in-residence. Each year, groups of scholars from Asia and America, sharing common interests and competent in diverse disciplinary techniques, will be assembled in Honolulu. Each scholar follows his own researches (and the scholar may bring with him some of his advanced graduate students for this purpose), but under the stimulation of discussions with his colleagues in other fields and from other countries.

The center seems likely to become the focal point in a vast network of academic relations over two continents. It is developing long-range agreements with other universities, both in the United States and Asia, by which a certain level of participation in the center's ongoing programs is guaranteed.

Such institutions as the East-West Center—or others of a character not yet discerned—may be increased in the years ahead. Their establishment may well facilitate fuller participation by alert universities in the cultural dimensions of international affairs.

Channels of Communication Between Government and Universities

Thus far in this chapter, a series of items illustrative of the cultural developments in American foreign policy and in federal activity which have taken place in recent decades has been presented. The AID and USIS programs, the work of the Office of Education, and the Peace Corps are representative of a new interrelationship among higher education, foreign policy, federal activity, and international affairs. Similar developments could be traced in the Department of Agriculture's activities having impact on education, and in the university work, particularly at the research level, made possible by the National Institutes of Health.

All branches of the defense services not only subsidize research in universities, carry on advanced educational programs of their own, and contract with colleges and universities for training services, but also, through their entire recruitment and manpower policies, have continuing and pervasive influence on academic institutions. A full inventory of the federal activities derived from international concerns and influential on higher education is beyond the scope of this volume, but enough has been presented to indicate a decided and powerful trend.

Certain university problems, which are only incidentally related to foreign policy and international concerns, arise out of the closer relationship of the institutions to government. During the last three decades, federal expenditures for research have increased almost beyond comprehension and research funds have been allocated to universities on an unprecedented basis. In this process the traditional balance of interests within academic life has in many cases been profoundly altered. Much has been written about the overemphasis within some universities on the academic fields into which research funds flow most readily. Fears have been expressed about the neglect of basic research in order to accommodate applied research.

It is doubtless true that many universities have on occasion thought of research or service contracts as traditional grants-in-aid. It is partly to avoid the mistakes and errors flowing from this concept that earlier sections of this volume have emphasized that universities should undertake such contracts only when they are within the resources and balanced interests of the university. It is at this point that, so far as funds related to the international interests of the government are concerned, the development of university over-all policy is of utmost consequence.[11] That policy

[11] For an illustration of one institution's analysis of this problem see *Harvard and the Federal Government: A Report to the Faculties and Governing Boards of Harvard University* (Cambridge, Mass.: Harvard University, 1961), 36 pp.

must discern for each institution what it will not try to do as well as what it will undertake.

A critical factor in this entire area is the point at which university and government are in communication. A few of the nation's universities, either by the pre-eminence of their scholars in certain fields or by administrative initiative or both, are in direct and regular contact with governmental agencies. Some of these institutions maintain their own offices in Washington; many have designated officers who travel frequently to the Capital. In addition, a variety of associations, with headquarters in Washington, serve as liaison between their institutional members and the government. The Association of State Universities and Land-Grant Colleges and the newly established Association of University Graduate Schools are cases in point. In particular, the American Council on Education serves a notable role as the spokesman of higher education in Washington, and as the disseminator of information about governmental programs to the colleges and universities. In a recent reorganization of the Council, its Commission on International Education has become one of five central policy-determining groups. Under the commission is grouped a number of continuing committees which deal with particular aspects of international interests. The commission facilitates the representation of the academic community to the government and reports to that community on governmental and foundation activities in international affairs.

All of these channels of communication should remain open, and doubtless will be utilized in increasing degree. Additional channels are also needed, as was pointed out in the Morrill report by the Committee on the University and World Affairs. Particularly needed is an agency, advisory in nature, which will study continuously the role of higher education in world affairs and take the initiative in suggesting appropriate lines of development. In the report, *The University and World Affairs,* issued in late 1960, the committee concluded that:

What is especially needed is a new organization, based upon American universities and colleges, but able to take into account broad national needs. It would provide a mechanism through which universities and colleges can consider together educational planning, the development and employment of educational competence in world affairs, and the systematic cumulation and appraisal of growing educational experience in world affairs. It would facilitate communication for these same ends with agencies of government, business and foundations in the United States, and with the institutions of other nations.

In relation to the government, the organization would provide a source of independent and authoritative advice on matters such as the development of educational institutions abroad, educational exchange, and the support of American university programs for developing American competence. Government funds allocated for these purposes, however, should be made available directly to the educational institutions, which would accept responsibility individually or in cooperation.

The prestige of the organization would help, where such help were needed, to inspire confidence in other countries receiving United States governmental aid that the aid was being given for sound educational purposes. It would likewise tend to encourage the United States government to relax its close administrative supervision and legal controls over university participation in government-supported programs.[12]

As a result of this recommendation, a new organization called "Education and World Affairs" has been created. Chartered under the laws of New York State in 1962, and supported by major foundations, the organization began operation in April 1963. Its tasks, as stated in its charter, are:

To mobilize the resources of the educational community in the fullest possible development of American competence in world affairs.

To encourage the improvement and expansion of the existing network of international exchange in students, research, and ideas.

To promote the highest degree of international cooperation in education and the advancement of education in other nations.

Education and World Affairs (EWA) will conduct studies, hold

[12] Pp. 77–78.

conferences, formulate policy recommendations. It is not a fund-granting agency, but will serve as an independent voice of American universities in conversation with universities abroad and in the relations of the government with academic matters. With Herman B Wells as chairman of the EWA board, and under the executive presidency of William W. Marvel, the new agency is likely to become a major communication center and influence in the relations among American institutions, foreign universities, and governments.[13]

With creative leadership for responsible institutions of higher education at the national level and with continued improvement in the governmental machinery concerned with education, science, and culture in international matters, great achievement may be expected in this area. But to these two forward steps—dramatized by the creation of Education and World Affairs and the establishment of an effective coordinating Bureau of Cultural Affairs in the Department of State—a third must still be added. As has been emphasized in earlier pages of this volume, each college and university must formulate its own policy on reactions to the impact of world affairs. EWA may well facilitate this process, may provide a series of situation papers for the consideration of academic faculties and government officers, but only as individual institutions discern their own role with increasing clarity and responsibility will adequate achievement be gained.

[13] Offices of Education and World Affairs are located at 522 Fifth Ave., New York 36, N.Y. Trustees of the organization are Ellsworth Bunker, Ray R. Eppert, T. Keith Glennan, Robert Goheen, John A. Hannah, Kenneth Holland, Douglas M. Knight, David E. Lilienthal, William W. Marvel (president), Frank McCulloch, Franklin D. Murphy (vice-chairman), Herman B Wells (chairman), and Logan Wilson.

5

International Exchange of Academic Personnel

THE IMPORTANCE OF interchange of academic persons, both at the student and faculty level and for all types of institutions of higher education, has been stressed in the discussions throughout this volume. Exchange of persons is the continuing base of cultural relations among nations, and the processes and programs and problems of such exchange deserve much more systematic study than they have yet received.

Scholars, young and old, have been travelers since the beginnings of higher education. The wandering scholars of the Middle Ages, and particularly of the Renaissance and the early years of European universities, came in contact with the cultural forces of all their Western world. And they did so untrammeled and unaided by passports, visas, health certificates, currency regulations, foundation programs, or scholarships. The great university centers of learning have attracted men from divers cultures through the ages.

In the twentieth century, however, the movement abroad of scholars, young and old, has reached proportions never before known. Governmental regulations and facilities have organized and channeled all interchange more carefully than ever before, even though governments have actually financed or sponsored a very small proportion of the interchange. Programs, both public and private, to aid particular types of exchange have been created on a phenomenal scale in the present century. These programs, ranging from the Rhodes Scholarships to the Fulbright

Fellowships, from foundation programs to scholarships for religious groups and to the Peace Corps, are central to the impact of world affairs on higher education and to the role of cultural affairs in international relations. The interchange of persons across national boundary lines is essential to the advancement of scholarship and to political policy; such exchange is both an objective and a technique of modern life.

Institutions of higher education themselves have welcomed foreign students, professors, research specialists, and visitors on an unprecedented scale in recent decades. Special programs of study for foreigners have been established widely in Europe, in some areas of Asia, and in North America. As has been earlier pointed out, a new sensitivity to the problem of foreign students has led throughout the United States to the establishment of special advisory services for them, to the formulation of a new professional association of foreign student advisers, to the creation of community groups of citizens interested in the welfare of foreign groups. We are today conscious of the human, political, and academic problems and potentials of interchange as never before.

Foreign Students in the United States

Although the records are not very exact, it is estimated that about 7,000 foreign students were registered at colleges and universities in the United States in 1925, and that there were 10,000 by 1931. The numbers declined somewhat during the depression and war years, but have risen dramatically since World War II, as is evidenced in Table 1. In the table are data, drawn from the census annually made by the Institute of International Education, concerning the total number of foreign students registered in American colleges and universities each year between 1949–50 and 1961–62. The area of origin of the students is shown, indicating the nationality pattern of those who come to America. Relative proportions of undergraduate and graduate students are indicated. In the academic year 1961–62, the number of foreign students in the United States reached an all-time high; there were 58,086 students from 149 countries or areas studying in 1,798 United States institutions of higher education. The number has been increasing every year since the war, in three of these years it increased by 10 or more percent. The number increased by 119 percent between 1950 and 1962. If this rate of increase continues through the 1960's, we shall register some 132,000 college and university students from outside the United States in 1970.

To a considerable extent these students come from areas of the world where institutions of higher education are in short supply and where new nations are emerging. The great growth in numbers of students has come from the Far East, the Near and Middle East, and in recent years from Africa. The numbers of students from Europe, from Canada, and from parts of Latin America are relatively stable. Within the United States, foreign students are much more widely distributed now than in earlier years; although about a fourth of the visiting students are still registered in the institutions of three states—California, New York, and Michigan—no state is without foreign students and almost every campus has at least a few students. Seventeen institutions have more than 500 foreign students each, but in only nine institutions do foreign students account for as much as 5 percent of the total registration. Howard University with 16.1 percent of its students from outside the United States and Massachusetts Institute of Technology with 12.3 percent are unusual in this respect; on most campuses fewer than 1 percent of the students are from abroad. In 1962 about 30 percent of all foreign students were self-supporting; about 9 percent received financial help from the United States Government; other governments, foundations, and private organizations helped to support many others, but a very large number of students were here on their own or family support. As to fields of study, the 1962 proportions are fairly typical for recent years—22 percent of the students were in engineering, 19 percent in the humanities, 16 percent in the natural and physical sciences, 14 percent in the social sciences, and diminishing proportions

Table 1: Foreign Students in United States Colleges and Universities: 1949–62 *

Academic Year	Total No. Foreign Students in U.S.	Annual Percentage Increase	Area of Origin†								Academic Status‡		
			Far East	Latin America	Europe	North America	Near and Middle East	Africa	Oceania	Soviet Union	Undergraduates	Graduates	Percentage Undergraduates§
1949–50	26,433	....	6,429	6,023	5,544	4,421	2,357	904	200	30	13,295	8,895	50
1950–51	29,813	13	7,314	6,409	7,102	4,553	2,990	1,027	217	55	14,636	8,851	49
1951–52	30,462	2	7,280	6,734	7,117	4,299	3,421	1,072	251	43	14,902	9,201	40
1952–53	33,675	9	8,129	7,615	7,856	4,572	3,998	1,081	316	80	18,185	15,501	54
1953–54	33,833	.005	8,675	8,478	6,171	4,845	4,101	1,163	354	....	17,583	15,250	52
1954–55	34,232	1	9,838	8,446	5,196	4,714	4,416	1,234	337	9	19,124	12,110	50
1955–56	56,494	7	11,202	8,474	5,502	5,042	4,662	1,231	353	2	20,668	13,632	37
1956–57	40,666	12	12,949	9,110	5,996	5,444	5,243	1,424	424	9	22,662	14,229	55
1957–58	43,391	7	14,206	9,212	6,816	5,334	5,695	1,515	495	21	23,502	15,118	54
1958–59	47,245	9	15,823	10,249	6,601	5,512	6,619	1,735	612	5	24,349	16,793	52
1959–60	48,486	3	17,175	9,428	6,362	5,761	7,110	1,959	568	30	24,975	18,682	55
1960–61	53,107	10	19,222	9,626	6,686	6,128	7,862	2,831	658	16	26,632	21,404	50
1961–62	58,086	9	21,568	9,915	6,833	6,639	8,277	3,930	796	37	29,376	24,624	51

* The figures for Table 1 are drawn from the annual census of foreign students reported by the Institute of International Education. The reports began in 1947–48, and were issued under the title *Education for One World* for seven years; beginning in 1954–55 the reports are titled *Open Doors*. The census has become increasingly comprehensive. Data for the years 1948–54 are corrected in terms of the regional groupings used after 1954.

† Area figures do not include stateless students.

‡ Figures not included for special or unclassified students.

§ Of total number of foreign students in the United States.

in business administration, medicine, education, and agriculture.

A 1962 report prepared for the American Assembly of Columbia University indicates:

There has been a great deal of wishful thinking both in the colleges and in government, about these foreign students. In the early postwar years, particularly, the necessity of providing a good education was seriously compromised with the desire to win friends for America. Too frequently, colleges received foreign students in a gesture of friendship, and modified standards of achievement to meet the circumstances. Some students returned home with memories of a happy sojourn but not too much in the way of effective education. Others were baffled by the adjustments to a different cultural milieu, irritated by collegiate restrictions or by the "red tape" of visa and financial operations. While most students seem to have profited by their American visit, the results are not invariably advantageous for the individual student or conducive for friendship for America. In the last decade, however, there have been marked improvements in the selection and reception of foreign students, in counseling them on academic matters, in adjusting them to American living, and in adherence to standards in estimating their achievement. Few universities are now without a foreign student adviser who is professional in his approach to his tasks.[1]

In spite of the decade of improvement reported here, a 1962 statement issued by the Committee on Educational Interchange Policy of the Institute of International Education points out that

Perhaps a third of the 58,000 foreign students at American educational institutions in 1962 were thoroughly screened to make sure they had the academic preparation, the language proficiency, and the financial support necessary to a successful study experience. Another third were partially screened at some point in the exchange process and a final third probably had no screening at all. Thus between one-third and two-thirds of the foreign students coming to the United States today are in some degree deficient in knowledge of what they will find, where they will find it, what preparation they need, and how much it will cost.[2]

[1] Robert Blum (ed.), *Cultural Affairs and Foreign Relations* (Englewood Cliffs, N.J.: Prentice-Hall, Inc., 1963), pp. 85–86.

[2] Committee on Educational Interchange Policy, *A Foreign Student Program for the Developing Countries During the Coming Decade* (New York: Institute of International Education, 1962), p. 2.

With the numbers of foreign applicants increasing, with the explosive growth in American colleges and universities which characterizes the 1960's because of trends in American population, and with the present inadequacies in selection and treatment of foreign students, it is obvious that severe problems of policy and coordination lie ahead. Should we continue to admit large numbers of foreign students? If so, on what basis of selection and to what programs of study? Such questions must be considered in both political and academic terms, and they must be considered in the 1960's more seriously than ever before.

The United States, at present, has in its native student body about a third of all the college and university students in the world. And about a fourth of all students studying outside their own country are studying in the United States. These foreign students in the United States account for a smaller proportion of our total registrations than is the case in Germany, Great Britain, France, and probably Russia. These comparisons do not provide an answer to the number we should receive, although they lead some analysts of the situation to the conviction that we should receive larger numbers than are now coming. The decision as to number actually lies in what contribution we can make to the educational development of capable individuals—a vital part of the American democratic dream; what repercussions would arise from restriction on numbers; and, by no means least, as has been emphasized earlier, what contributions foreign students make to our own campuses and to the education of the American students with whom they associate. In general, considerations based on these factors lead to the conclusion that we must and should continue to receive large numbers of foreign students. The estimate of 132,000 probable registrants by 1970 is not an unreasonable or undesirable figure. It is particularly important that such numbers come because contact with them is a vital part of the education of young American citizens faced with twentieth-century responsibilities.

Yet it is not total numbers that are of paramount concern. Are we getting the best selection of foreign students? To quote again from the American Assembly report:

Recognizing fully the varieties of pre-college education found in different cultures, American colleges and universities should make certain that applicants for admission are in the upper percentiles of ability within the groups from which they come. For the very able, financial help should be available; admission of foreign students should not hinge upon financial status. But to admit the less able, though it be humane, is to risk the frustrations of personal failure and to weaken United States prestige in the competition among nationals trained in different societies. In the context of the cold war, it is more advantageous for the United States to be represented by able returnees than by less able former students. The standards for admission and achievement in American colleges and universities are likely to become more rigorous in the coming decade, and must be made so for foreign as well as for American students. Selective recruitment of particularly talented young men and women should be a basic principle in American reception of foreign students, adhered to rigorously as the population pressures for place in higher education become greater.[8]

Selection of foreign students must be more careful, must focus on the abilities of these students, not only abstract intellectual abilities but the particular qualities and competencies needed by their own societies and requisite to the specific educational programs to be undertaken in the United States. In determining policy and practice concerning the selection and training of students for an American sojourn, each college or university has a deep responsibility. But it is also likely that the Federal Government must be involved in policy determination, in facilitation and coordination without control, and in program financing to an increasing extent.

One critical factor demanding early attention, mentioned earlier, is the provision of services for counseling and testing prospective foreign students before they leave their own country.

[8] Blum, *op. cit.*, p. 87. See also *The College, the University, and the Foreign Student*, report of a Committee on the Foreign Student in American Colleges and Universities of the National Association of Foreign Student Advisers, 500 Riverside Drive, New York, 1963; 26 pp.

Tests of proficiency in language, of background training adequate for the program sought by a student, together with academic and personal counseling in the student's own country, may prevent infinite frustrations and failures. The Institute of International Education now has a series of regional offices abroad which might well take leadership in the establishment and operation of these needed services. But in addition to these offices, the resources of upgraded education attachés in key United States embassies and of academic and organizational personnel stationed abroad must be utilized and coordinated. It is probable that the provision of such services should remain under the management of nongovernmental agencies, such as the Institute of International Education, but governmental cooperation and support are essential if such services are to be maintained on anything like an adequate basis.

Certain factors concerning the foreign students coming to the United States should be observed. At what age should students come? There has been in recent years heavy emphasis on the graduate, postbaccalaureate level in many organized exchange programs (as, for example, the Fulbright program), but even so, the proportion of graduate students, as seen in Table 1, has not increased substantially during the past decade. The great number of foreign students continues to be at the college, undergraduate level. A smaller, but growing number of secondary school pupils are exchanged. It may well be that, during the coming decade, the proportion of secondary and of graduate students may increase. But any evaluation of the proportions rests upon increased clarity of the purposes specific interchanges are intended to serve. In general terms, secondary exchanges seem to result primarily in good will for the United States; college students focus on general education, though with a very large emphasis on vocational training within the framework of general education; graduate students direct their major attention to work on their specialization.

In exchanges at all these levels consistent and constant attention should be given to fitting the student and his program together. Too many foreign students, as has been pointed out, know too little about American institutions of higher education to make wise choices among them. They try to flock to name institutions, or are guided quite loosely to institutions where good programs along their lines of interest may or may not be found. More effective counseling and guidance services are of great importance. Within the United States most colleges and universities should, to the degree possible, follow a policy of selective recruitment in reaching out for foreign students who can profitably pursue their established programs. In this connection, it seems likely that the junior colleges of the United States should receive a much larger proportion of America's foreign students than they now do. The junior colleges provide terminal programs of major value to large numbers of students coming from rapidly developing countries, and at the same time may provide, in their academic programs, an excellent initiation into American higher education.

United States Students Abroad

The Institute of International Education reports in *Open Doors* for 1962 that 19,836 United States students were enrolled in 590 institutions located in 66 foreign countries in the 1960–61 academic year. This number represents an increase of 30 percent over the preceding year. The largest number of these were in Mexico, but France, Canada, the United Kingdom, Germany, Austria, Switzerland, and Vatican City each received more than a thousand students from the United States. Almost two-thirds of the total were in Europe. Whereas 38 percent of the foreign students in the United States come from the Far East, only 5 percent of the United States students outside the country were in the Far East. Almost half of the Americans abroad were studying in the fields of, first, the humanities; next, the medical sciences; third, the social sciences; less than 10 percent were in the physical and natural sciences.

Most of the undergraduates abroad—many of whom limit their foreign student sojourn to one year—are privately financed. Many of them are resident in foreign centers maintained by American colleges and universities for Junior Year Abroad programs. This group seems likely to grow rapidly since an increasing number of American institutions are establishing such foreign centers, often in direct cooperation with universities abroad. A considerable proportion of the group abroad are graduate students, many working on their dissertations. Government grants, in a variety of forms and programs, are a substantial (though by no means adequate) financial support for these advanced students.

Many of the questions on policy and practice that were raised in respect to foreign students within the United States should also be raised about United States students abroad. Are our students, in adequate numbers, going to the right places to study the things most important for the advancement of American scholarship and the national interest? Are the students who go our best choices as investment in foreign study? Are the programs for study abroad of these students effectively related to their academic careers at home? To the general interests of American scholarship? To what extent are the charges true that some of the American off-campus centers abroad are only "American islands" in a foreign culture, examples of a sort of academic extraterritoriality? Relatively little actual research has been completed on American students abroad. Analysis of Americans' educational experience abroad, and its effect on students, on universities, and on the relations between the United States and other countries, is highly desirable.

Exchange of Scholars

Just as there has been an emphasis on foreign study at the graduate student level in recent years, there has also been an increase in the exchange of postgraduate scholars, either as faculty members or in connection with advanced research. In 1962, reports the Institute of International Education, the United States received 5,530 scholars from 90 countries, who were affiliated for the year with 390 American colleges or universities. In the same year 2,427 American faculty members were on assignments in 90 foreign countries. These members represent substantial increases over preceding years. In view of the population growth in American higher education and the shortage of teaching staff—a shortage likely to become acute in the 1960's—it may be difficult to continue to send large numbers of faculty members abroad, and it may be increasingly desirable to recruit much larger numbers of foreign faculty members as visiting professors. Certainly the total number of exchanges at the faculty and research level will increase substantially over the coming decade.

The geographical areas within which this interchange takes place present an interesting pattern, as indicated in Table 2. Prior to 1962 considerably more than half of the American scholars going abroad went to Europe; it seems probable that the coming decade will witness a considerably greater dispersion than that for 1962. Within the United States the University of California and Harvard University each received more than 400 of these scholars

TABLE 2

EXCHANGE OF SCHOLARS BETWEEN THE UNITED STATES AND WORLD AREAS IN 1961-62 *

Geographic Area	Percent of Foreign Scholars to United States (N = 5,530)	Percent of U.S. Scholars to Foreign Areas (N = 2,427)
Europe	41.0	50
Far East	34.0	16
Latin America	9.0	10
Near and Middle East	7.0	8
Canada	4.0	1
Africa	2.1	7

* Tables 2 and 3 are based on data reported in Institute of International Education, *Open Doors* (1962), pp. 12, 14, 29.

in 1962; Massachusetts Institute of Technology received more than 300; the University of Minnesota received more than 200; and 9 additional universities each received more than 100. Only 2 American universities—Michigan State and California—had as many as 100 of their own faculty members abroad during 1962.

The fields of specialization covered by this interchange also indicate an interesting pattern, as shown in Table 3. The factors responsible for this pattern are obviously more than those of academic interest and need. They include political and financial considerations as well as prestige factors. The pattern needs to be studied in its relation to the needs of American higher education.

TABLE 3

FIELDS OF SPECIALIZATION OF VISITING SCHOLARS AND UNITED STATES SCHOLARS ABROAD, 1962

Field of Specialization	Percent of Foreign Scholars to United States (N = 5,530)	Percent of U.S. Scholars to Foreign Areas (N = 2.427)
Natural and physical sciences	44.3	19.6
Medicine	20.2	8.8
Humanities	12.9	27.6
Social sciences	9.3	22.6
Engineering	8.0	5.6
Agriculture	2.5	4.8
Education	2.2	7.7
Business administration	0.6	3.3
Total	100.0	100.0

In general the exchange of scholars is probably more thoughtfully planned and managed than is the exchange of students. Many of the exchanges are arranged in terms of carefully conceived programs sponsored by foundations and by governments; all the interchanges are undertaken by the institutions involved with attention to the known needs and achievements of scholarly fields and of individual persons.

There can be no doubt that these exchanges, on the whole, benefit the individual scholars and the institutions involved and that they contribute to the general advancement of knowledge. In most cases, the scholarly foreign sojourn is also an important cultural experience. Certainly the American faculty members who have served as scholars and research workers abroad bring back to their own campuses not only new achievements in their specializations but new insights into cultures observed and into international relations. Yet it must also be recognized that continuing appraisal of the policies and procedures of interchange at this advanced level is seriously needed, particularly as we move into one of the most difficult decades in the history of American higher education. From what geographic areas and in what scholarly and professional fields do we need to bring foreign specialists, and, conversely, which American scholars can most advantageously sojourn abroad, and where?

The Need for Research and Policy Analysis

As one studies our reception of foreign students, the dispatch of young Americans for study abroad, and the interchange of scholars, professional specialists, and research workers, he becomes increasingly aware of the need for basic, over-all policy formulation. A paramount need for the immediate future is the discernment of guidelines which can increase the scope and the efficiency of the interchange movement. It will be impossible for us to admit all the students who want an American sojourn, or to send all the Americans who want to study abroad. What are the principles on which we may admit—or selectively recruit—foreign students on a basis equivalent to the tightened-up admission policies now in process of development for American students? Wise selection requires clearly established criteria which, for foreign students, must involve both academic considerations, the manpower needs of nations, the policies of governments, and the democratic commitment to individual growth through educational opportunity. The same considerations apply to the American students enabled to spend periods of study abroad.

The formulation of wise policy requires a good deal of critical analysis of the experience this country and others have already had with exchange of academic persons. Until recently this analyzed experience was lacking, but since World War II an increasing body of research literature on exchange has been appearing. Many of these studies are in the form of master's theses or doctoral dissertations. Many are in the files of governmental agencies. The early studies are almost exclusively descriptive, often simply tabulating the reactions of groups of students to their foreign experience. Contributions to this literature are also appearing in the form of personal essays or memoirs or philosophical analyses written by individuals about their educational sojourn outside their own country. Returned Fulbrighters have written in this fashion.

In the early 1950's a more systematic and scientific approach to the field was undertaken under the auspices of the Social Science Research Council. With foundation financing, the council sponsored four pairs of studies, each pair focused on the American visits of students from one of four countries—Sweden, Mexico, India, and Japan. In each pair, one study was made of students then registered in certain United States universities, and another study was made in historical depth, through interviews with representative returnees to the country. These studies, published in a series of volumes, constitute the best analyses of conditions and results of interchange which have as yet been made.[4] A general analysis of all the findings in these studies, cast in an anthropological frame, was made by Cora Du Bois under the title *Foreign Students and Higher Education in the United States* and published in the series of which the present book is the concluding volume. Noteworthy in Dr. Du Bois' volume is her tentative analy-

[4] For a list of volumes in this series of studies, see p. 15, n. 13.

sis of prearrival attitudes of students, of the successive stages of adjustment and readjustment through which they move, and of the influence of personality factors in these stages and in the total reaction to the experience.

It is unfortunate that the research program of the Social Science Research Council in this field was not continued, although a significant number of individual studies have appeared since that time. There is now more recorded information about exchanges, as in the annual census reports of the Institute of International Education, than has been adequately coordinated and interpreted. Further research is, of course, needed, particularly of a sociological and educational nature, but even equally urgent is the focusing of what is now known, or can be learned, on the issues of general policy which must be faced.

There are, of course, various groups working on policy questions. The Board of Foreign Scholarships, set up to direct the Fulbright program, has of necessity been concerned with policy for the operations it directs. Emphasis in the Fulbright program on the exchange of advanced scholars and graduate students is a policy decision of wide consequence. The board has repeatedly formulated policy decisions out of the concrete issues placed before it, as have all governmental agencies, foundations, and organizations concerned with the field. Under the 1961 Fulbright-Hays Act the board's responsibilities in policy formulation are increased to deal with the total interests of the government in exchange over and beyond its interest in those for whom it is financially responsible. In this enlarged function we may anticipate the formulation of policy recommendations by the board for general consideration as well as for the conduct of its own operations.

In 1954, a review of the operations of the Institute of International Education recommended that the institute concern itself more thoroughly with continuing research and policy suggestion. As a result the institute established a Committee on Educational

Exchange Policy charged with (1) clarifying the values of exchanges, (2) suggesting standards and objectives for exchange activities, (3) identifying problems and suggesting solutions, and (4) identifying promising programs. The committee published fifteen pamphlet reports between 1955 and 1962.[5] These are important statements, and several of them, notably the first and the last of those listed, are worthy of extensive and careful consideration. Able people, widely representative, have served on the committee, but they meet only briefly four times a year and the provision of an adequate research and drafting secretariat for the committee is difficult. Although the committee does not set policy for the institute, to a considerable degree its reports deal with matters in which the institute is operationally involved. As in the case of the Board of Foreign Scholarships, the institute's policy-study group is too limited in its concerns. In many respects, probably the highest level of policy analysis can be reached only if organizational and operational influences or interests are kept at a minimum. Every agency active in educational exchange must, of course, study its own operations—the equivalent of institutional research for the university—and adopt policies as a part of administrative procedure, but an external agency, outside the channel of administrative responsibility, may be needed to formulate over-all appraisals and policy recommendations.

[5] The reports, available free of charge through the Publications Division, Institute of International Education, 800 Second Ave., New York 17, N.Y., carry the following titles: *The Goals of Student Exchange* (1955); *Geographic Distribution of Exchange Programs* (1956); *Chinese Students in the United States, 1948-1955* (1956); *Orientation of Foreign Students* (1956); *Expanding University Enrollments and the Foreign Students* (1957); *Hungarian Refugee Students and United States Colleges and Universities* (1957); *United States Medical Training for Foreign Students and Physicians* (1957); *The Foreign Student: Exchangee or Immigrant?* (1958); *Hungarian Refugee Students and United States Colleges and Universities: One Year Later* (1958); *Academic Exchanges with the Soviet Union* (1958); *Twenty Years of United States Government Programs in Cultural Relations* (1959); *College and University Programs of Academic Exchange* (1960); *African Students in the United States* (1960); *Educational Exchange in the Economic Development of Nations* (1961); *A Foreign Student Program for the Developing Countries during the Coming Decade* (1962).

It is suggested therefore that a National Committee on Educational Exchange Policy should be established under appropriate auspices. While the institute's committee is in many ways excellent, it is possible that its functions should be taken over by a continuing committee under the newly established Education and World Affairs, Inc. The policy committee, composed of outstanding citizens, including government and organization personnel acting in their individual capacities, should have a secretariat capable of conducting studies, contracting for research, and drafting manuscripts for the committee's consideration. It should function very much as the Educational Policies Commission set up by the National Education Association and the American Association of School Administrators has functioned. The cooperation of government and foundations would be essential in establishing and financing the committee. The committee should avoid all operational activities. The government, however, could well contract with it for special studies and reports, could make grants to provide a share of its annual cost, and should ensure the careful consideration of committee reports and statements by all governmental divisions concerned.

It should be recognized immediately that in recent years the Federal Government has markedly improved its own machinery for research and policy formulation. As reported earlier, an Advisory Commission was established under the Fulbright-Hays Act of 1961, to which various studies and policy questions have already been referred. The Commission early conducted a study on American artistic presentations abroad. Its first annual report, issued at the end of March 1963, is the most careful and comprehensive report on government-financed exchange of persons which has yet appeared.[6] It covers the period 1949–62, inclusive, during which the Department of State financed foreign sojourns (as students, lecturers, researchers, teachers, and spe-

[6] The United States Advisory Commission on International Educational and Cultural Affairs, *A Report to Congress on the Effectiveness of the Educational and Cultural Exchange Program of the United States Department of State*, Mimeographed. March 29, 1963. 60 pp.

cialists) for 21,412 Americans, and American sojourns for 52,773 persons from abroad. The Commission and its staff secured reports and analyses from former grantees in 20 countries, from 131 officers attached to 22 United States embassies and consulates, and from a wide range of informed observers of the interchange process.

The report to Congress emphasizes that the exchange program is and has been extraordinarily effective as "an essential and valuable part of America's total international effort." It presents evidence that the interchanges have increased mutual understanding, succeeded in reducing "many misconceptions and ugly stereotypes about the American people," provided educational experiences useful to individuals and to the countries concerned, opened up channels of communication and "strongly supported one of the nation's most basic international objectives—of helping support strong free societies able to work together in mutual trust and understanding on the grave issues of our time."

Suggestions for improvement were also put forward by the Commission. It felt that we should attract more promising and able foreign students in the have-not rather than the elite groups and that we should "make a particular effort to seek out and select those candidates abroad who are sufficiently vigorous and restless to help promote desirable social and economic change." The establishment of field selection centers, under private auspices but with government support, is recommended for all areas from which we receive students. The Commission felt that the amount of individual grants should be increased, even at the risk of reducing the number of grants, in order to attract the ablest persons from abroad and to send the ablest Americans abroad. It recommended nation-by-nation rather than over-all program planning and pointed out that "the new enthusiasm for work with developing nations should not lead to neglect or downgrading of the educational and cultural programs with Europe." It recommended special studies of the role of cultural affairs officers in American embassies and additional study of possibilities of administrative coordination.

The Commission's work, of course, covered only one segment of the total range of interchange of persons and was broadly administrative rather than psychological or sociological in character. It provides a model, however, for what needs to be done on an even wider scale, and in greater depth. The Committee, while composed of private individuals, operated as a public agency. Its work will doubtless be continued and expanded as a policy-recommending body. Its operations should, as closely as possible, be coordinated with such nongovernmental agencies as the new organization Education and World Affairs.

The role of the government should be that of assuring continuing study and policy recommendation by an independent agency, linking government with institutions of higher education and with organizations dealing with exchange programs. By such support, the government can encourage the widest range of policy consideration and the continuing conduct of research in an area presently neglected. The government can then shape its own programs in the light of reasonable over-all planning and expand its funds in increasingly effective measure and on what is likely to be an expanding scale. In financing the proposed committee, under contract with its sponsoring agency, the government would be supporting the highest level of analysis for its own operations and the most comprehensive effort of cooperation among private agencies as well as between those agencies and the government.

Interchange of Persons Between Government and University

A problem of governmental-university relations over and beyond that concerned with exchange of persons is that of government use of university personnel and—the neglected reverse side of the same coin—university use of government personnel. The path between university campus and government office is well traveled in this generation, and a considerable share of the traveling arises from the impact of world affairs.

During recent decades most universities have had to revise their leave-of-absence policies to provide for periods of temporary government service for members of their faculties. More recently those universities which have contracted with such agencies as AID for overseas service or which have established campuses abroad have had to make provision for tours of overseas duty of faculty members without hardship to their tenure, promotion, and retirement rights. As we move into a decade of serious shortages in faculty personnel, the machinery for these arrangements is likely to be more efficient but leaves themselves may be more difficult to arrange, yet such leaves are a part of the situation which give universities a growing partnership in world affairs and which continually push forward the frontiers of learning. Faculty exchanges and leaves cannot be decreased without the danger of academic provincialism and without serious handicap to the government. It may well be necessary for universities which take a particularly active part in international enterprises to carry on their rosters larger faculties than they regularly use, in expectation that a given proportion of the whole will be on unpaid leave of absence for work in government or industry, foreign or domestic. One major university already calculates, on the basis of a decade of experience, that 10 percent of its faculty will be away each year and has enlarged its roster accordingly.

Reference has already been made in this volume to the desirability of the government utilizing academic personnel on leave from their home post for duty in connection with most phases of the educational, scientific, and cultural areas of foreign operations. It has been suggested, too, that the criteria for academic and governmental promotions, so far as posts related to education, science, and culture are concerned, should and could be more effectively coordinated than they now are. With an emphasis in most universities on research and publication as criteria of status, and with the need for continuing, objective appraisal of operations in the cultural field as great as it is, government personnel policies and regulations could well move in the direction of encouraging research and reasonable publication by its borrowed staff, as free as feasible from the limitations of classified material.

Providing greater opportunities for academic personnel to do the things while in government service which will add to their standing within the home academic community, however, will not increase, and might decrease, the number of scholars available to man the expanding universities of this decade. Greater use in academic institutions of government personnel "on home leave" would, on the other hand, help alleviate faculty shortages in selected areas and might enrich the university programs, particularly in area studies and in certain professional fields. It has been indicated in this volume that the personnel concerned with educational, scientific, and cultural activities in our embassies throughout the world should be expanded and upgraded, and they should also have a closer relation with American universities. On home leave, regular members of the foreign service could well be assigned to universities for limited periods of service, particularly in the instructional and research programs of world area centers. An educational attaché, returned from duty in a Latin American nation, could well be attached for a semester to the Latin American program of the University of Texas, for example, enriching the program of that center from his personal experience, reorienting himself to the changing conditions of American academic life, and helping by his presence and counsel, to interrelate more closely the Federal Government and the university in this total program.

In this connection the government and the universities may well take a leaf from the book of experience of the American Field Service program. In this program a group of specialists are stationed as observers and analysts in various areas of the world and are periodically returned home to serve as consultants to a group of cooperating universities. It might be advantageous to all concerned for our cultural or scientific or educational attachés to spend comparable periods in United States universities under a regular, cyclical arrangement. It could also advantageously be written into the contracts of diverse AID, USIS, and other agency personnel that a final period of their tour of duty be in an American university particularly concerned with the area in which they are stationed. Thus, the African Studies Center at the University of California, Los Angeles, could advantageously receive the director of the Peace Corps in Nigeria for a semester at the conclusion of his overseas assignment, even if he were not a regular member of the foreign service but were on leave of absence from another institution.

The possibilities for greater use of government personnel, not only as guest lecturers and consultants, but also as teachers and guides of research for graduate students should be carefully explored. The need for interrelation between government and academic personnel mounts as the pressure on American universities increases and as the role of universities in overseas enterprises expands. Imaginative and farsighted utilization of superior manpower resources for both universities and government are possible in this area.

It is obvious that, for all the purposes of cultural relations among nations, cultural qualities and resources are embodied in persons. Exchange of persons between countries, and between government and academic institutions within a country, is central to the responsibilities of contemporary education, science, and culture in international affairs. Within recent decades this exchange has been fostered on an unprecedented scale by both public and private agencies in this and in other countries. The exchange is likely to continue and increase, but the complexities and pressures which surround it are also increasing. The necessity for extensive and intensive research on the processes and conditions of exchange is today imperative, and such research must enter into continuing policy analysis and decision.

6

Responsibility and Opportunity

MOST OF THE pages of this brief volume have been based upon analysis of the impact of world affairs on American colleges and universities and of institutional reaction to that impact during the past half century. A pervasive historical trend has been observed, both toward the inclusion of education, science, and culture in foreign policy and toward a steadily rising academic interest and activity in international matters. There is a certain impersonality, a vast inevitability, about the trend. The impression should never be left, however, that the trend is so casual that an institution may or may not choose to be involved in it or, on the other hand, that the trend is so powerful and monolithic in its influence that the institution can do nothing about it. In reality, the trend toward involvement is strong and inevitable, but institutions, individually and in concert, may shape their actions under the impact. Academia in the free world has not lost the initiative, the power of shaping constructively its role in foreign policy and international affairs.

The difficulty lies not in the trend, which produces both opportunities and responsibilities, but in the unthoughtful and opportunistic response of too many institutions. It is, as has been emphasized throughout this report, the lack of institutional policy which is bad. To receive foreign students or to make recommendations for Fulbright awards purely by chance, to develop an area study under the wave of an untested popularity, to seek an AID contract for the sake of its illusory budgetary administrative overhead or to open up a new program simply because a foundation grant can be found for it, to try to do too much or to choose at random what to do in the international field must inevitably lead to frustration, to dispersion of energies and resources, to a degradation of the independent responsibilities that inhere in academic institutions. We may ask of government continual analysis of its programs in education, science, and culture, may seek frequent administrative reconstructions or alterations in the regulations controlling its relations with colleges and universities. But the difficulties in those relations lie fully as much on the academic as on the governmental side.

The thesis here reiterated is that each college or university needs, at this stage, to inventory its resources and activities and experiences bearing on world affairs, to formulate with clarity its policies respecting developments of the proximate future with a view to what and how much the institution should do, and to provide an institutional structure—an office or an institute or a committee—which will coordinate the university's undertakings, continually appraise its activities, and be the focal point for continuing re-examination of policies and programs. To drift through the international currents of the twentieth century is not safe for any college or university. An academic plan built on an institution's strengths, avoiding overextension of activities, and recognizing the unique, twentieth-century interrelations of academic interests, foreign policy, government, and international affairs is now necessary for any institution which is responsible within its range of freedom.

In this volume and the preceding volumes of this series it has been stressed that academic planning needs to be both comprehensive and realistic. The college or university curriculum must be considered, not only in those courses and programs which deal directly with the subject of international relations, but in all the matters which prepare educated men and women for the realities embraced within our expanding world horizons—in languages, the sciences, history and literature, and the international dimensions of professional studies. The policy of an institution in respect to area studies, specialized training in international relations, and research needs to be envisaged in the light of institutional resources and of national needs. Extracurricular activities designed to create a collegiate environment conducive to enlightened citizenship cannot wisely be ignored. Carefully pondered participation in service enterprises financed by government or outside agencies, ranging from Peace Corps training to AID contracts and to defense research should be envisaged on a scale which enriches but does not distort the institution.[1] Policies for the selection of foreign students, for the most farsighted use of foreign scholarship and exchange opportunities, for the release of faculty members for periods of government and foundation service are needed on every American campus.

Chapter 2 of this volume suggests a series of questions which should enter into the policy analysis of a liberal arts college, and chapter 3 outlines the experience of a number of universities in their evaluation of policy-making and administrative procedures. Policy making involves a form of institutional self-appraisal; in it should be involved all of the forces on the campus affected by it. It should ultimately be comprehensive and interrelated, though it may be evolved in such separate segments as policy toward foreign students or analysis of contract research, study of the effects of federal financing or of the national need for a given area study. As the over-all framework of policy emerges, some appropriate form of institutional machinery should be evolved, not to centralize or strait-jacket the administration of divers activities envisaged within the total policy, but to exercise a coordinating influence and to maintain policy scrutiny as related to new situations. A variety of university practices in this matter have been reported in preceding pages; what is best for a given campus must be determined by that campus; certainly no more elaborate

[1] See Clarence W. Hunnicutt (ed.), *America's Emerging Role in Overseas Education* (Syracuse, N.Y.: University School of Education, 1962), 148 pp.

institutional machinery should be set up than is warranted by the policy and programs of a campus, but generally speaking most campuses at present are inadequately organized and coordinated in this area.

The maintenance of a vigorous and institutionally coordinated program of instruction, research, and service in matters bearing on international affairs is not automatic. One aspect both of policy making and of policy implementation, as well as of continued growth, is the development of campuswide comprehension of the range and character of activities in the field. The office or bureau or institute chiefly responsible for program coordination within policy, should regularly receive and distribute reports on campus activities; should periodically conduct a census of the international and foreign interests and competencies of faculty members, should alert specialists to opportunities for further developments in their fields, should regularly schedule campuswide open meetings for the presentation of reports covering the whole range of developments within the institution. Only by keeping a whole faculty well informed can the full wealth of its competencies be brought to bear on such scattered yet interrelated matters as curriculum changes, extracurricular programs, exchange of students and faculty members, contract developments in a variety of fields, research progress, and direct relations with extramural enterprises.

The policy and program of a given institution may be improved if national policies and over-all needs, problems, and possibilities are studied with greater clarity, comprehensiveness, and continuity than is now the case. As has been indicated earlier, the new organization, Education and World Affairs, can render enormous service, not only at the national level, but also in setting up guidelines and raising questions for the continuing consideration of individual institutions. Moreover, the new agency, and every national association of higher education must become more effective in the evolution of governmental policy respecting education, science, and culture in international relations. The academic forces, having put their own institutions in order and envisaged their partnership role in twentieth-century action, may take increasing initiative in the conversations out of which public policy is made.

American colleges and universities have a flexibility and an experimental bent which make it possible for them to adjust to the times, to weave into their instructional and research and service programs the international interests which loom large in our society. To the extent that colleges and universities face their twentieth-century social and political environment seriously and plan for academic developments which enable them to bring their distinctive resources into coordination with foreign policy and international concerns, they will have vitality and consequence in the future. The basic need remains a thoughtful appraisal of the role of higher education in world affairs, of the part each institution can and should play in that role. A considered and farsighted policy for interrelating campus and forum, worked at assiduously by every conscientious college and university as well as by agencies of government, is the need of current years.

Index